MANIPULATING
MAN

MANIPULATING MAN

From Democracy to Orwellian Control

DAVID BRENNAN

For contact & bulk purchases:
ManipulatingMan@Yahoo.com

Published by Teknon Publishing, Metairie Louisiana

ISBN Number: 978-0-9887614-0-7

*Acknowledgments: It is a pleasure to acknowledge the
professional copy-editing done by Sue Hatfield-Green.*

To setting the captives free...

Table of Contents

PART I

Democracy

CHAPTER ONE

The Great Dichotomy

There was a time in America when a man's mind was his own, allowed to develop naturally, often choosing to embrace beliefs passed down from his ancestors that had weathered the tests of time. In those days, the people who filled the streets of the nation possessed something that brought a sense of peace to society, a depth of character born from beliefs that had been sifted slowly over the course of centuries. They were free in mind and spirit, and ruled over their government and society like the masters of a great ship, guiding it toward a destination limited only by their wills.

But ever present were those seeking to control such freedom, guided by the dark hope of unfathomable power and wealth promised from such an exploit. They first appeared in the early days when colonists from Europe arrived on the untamed shores of North America. Over the course of time, their ideological offspring would remain watchful and diligent, faithfully waiting for the opportunity to assume possession over those they sought to control. Perhaps it was the European strain of aristocracy that followed some from Europe to the New World, never able to accept the notion that the masses could be masters of their own fate.

Such individuals have always been present within the societies of man, that type which possesses an insatiable need to control others. But as the New World was settled their efforts toward control, making it into an image of the aristocracy that controlled the Old World, failed. It is the need to control others that is the common chord which binds them into a collective from which flows a common political and social ideology-the *ideology of control*.

Frustratingly for them, their efforts were thwarted over the course of centuries by the stubborn presence of morals and social mores embraced by the masses, born of religious beliefs that refused to budge, giving no space for their collective despotic wills. But their time would finally arrive in the middle of the twentieth century, ironically, from the advance of technology.

Within the discovery of certain powerful new technology, mankind has experienced a *great dichotomy*. That is to say, a good side as well as a bad side. In many cases this dichotomy appears obvious only some years later, after time has allowed the smoke to clear and its overall impact on the masses to finally be seen. And because in many cases such advancements bring tremendous benefits, it takes a while for the realization to dawn on them that a new threat arrived alongside those benefits, one that could not exist before the advancement appeared on the scene.

Such an occurrence is evident in the development of pharmaceuticals, capable of alleviating an array of afflictions that have tormented man since his beginning. The *great dichotomy* is that drugs have also been used to enslave masses of people with addictions, contributing to a visible decay of society and much individual misery. It also has enabled small groups of individuals to control those so addicted. Then there is the tremendous scientific achievement of splitting the atom, and thus enabling its primordial energy to be released for the lighting of cities and enabling forms of medicine previously unheard of. But the dark side is that it also has destroyed entire cities, and could potentially lead to an Armageddon. And then there is mankind's move away from the horse-drawn carriage to the motorized vehicle, lifting great burdens from the shoulders of the weary and causing commerce to expand greatly. But that same advancement empowered the tyrant Adolf Hitler to create powerful motorized cannons, called tanks, allowing him to come within a breath of extinguishing the flame of the Old World. In that day, his nemesis, Winston Churchill, would recognize the *great dichotomy* in his best-known speech, "Their Finest Hour," fearing a "new Dark Age made more sinister, and perhaps more protracted, by the lights of perverted science."[1]

Indeed, as science and technology advance, unleashing nature's blessings upon man, occasionally it empowers dark forces that previously could find no traction, eventually allowing them to make their move for control. And so it is in the case of American democracy having fallen victim to an advancement of technology that it could not account for, allowing despotic forces to finally achieve their collective goal: the effective end of rule by the masses in North America. The term democracy is not used here to indicate a nation that holds elections, but a nation ruled by the masses. In that regard, there is little question that America ceased being such a democracy sometime in the waning decades of the twentieth century.

Since her birth as a nation, the idea of America has served as a beacon of liberty for the masses across the four corners of the world, just as it has been a thorn in the side of those seeking to control them. Having broken free from the direct control of British aristocracy, the revolution in the New World set an example for the masses in the Old, presenting the ruling aristocracy there with a temporary challenge. But that challenge would be overcome by those who had always ruled over them. Not by resisting the advances, but by embracing them with an eye on control and, thus, ushering in a new age of *manipulation*. It is a new form of tyranny that goes beyond the boundaries of the old, one enabled by new and powerful advances in technology, allowing their eventual control to encompass the entirety of man's being. Such control, never before dreamed of by dictators, has allowed entry into the mind and soul of man, consuming his free will with the ability of guiding him toward any form of thought desired. Churchill's feared "Dark Age" brought about by the lights of "perverted science" finally became reality.

It is this new form of tyranny that American democracy has fallen in to, one unknown since man's beginnings. It is new and exists only because of the *great dichotomy*, having come into existence from the invention of technology that enables the few to control the many. And as that technology has settled in over the course of just a few decades, it finally created an opportunity for the ideological ancestors of those who had always sought to control the masses to finally fulfill that lust. But, unlike the tyranny of old that utilized brute force, and thus was quite overt and identifiable in its nature, this new tyranny is insidious, and therefore more challenging to see in its true light.

This is the story of how such tyranny came about and its reach into the minds of the masses that has caused a new man to appear-one that is its inevitable product and having little in common with his ancestors. It is a man who could not exist before this time. But as with all tyranny, here too, within its dark structure, there is a vulnerability, or Achilles heel, if you will, that if struck a powerful blow will break its grip. One single blow, carefully placed, inevitably would lead to its complete downfall. And with its downfall, the nation would enter a new and unprecedented age of enlightenment and freedom.

This is the story of how true democracy departed the land of America, and the tyranny that now *manipulates* the masses toward another will. But to fully understand, we must go back to the beginning when the first footsteps of colonists from England appeared on the shores of North America. And along with them arrived that type of individual possessing an insatiable need to control others. But because a sturdy foundation existed, guiding the masses to become the most free and prosperous people in history, it prevented those seeking to control them from achieving their goal, until the *great dichotomy* appeared.

CHAPTER TWO

In The Beginning

There was a cool breeze in the air that morning. And as it blew across the deck of the great ship, it touched the faces of those gathered like the gentle kisses of nature. It was a reward, of sorts, after having crossed the vast Atlantic Ocean, only to arrive at a place of utter wilderness. For many on board, the fear that the ship might not make it across the great expanse of sea, leaving them, and it, at the deep bottom, was finally relieved. But as that fear began to subside, a new one quickly took its place. In every direction along the virgin coast of North America, a thick forest blanketed the landscape. Although the lumber harvested from such a bounty could provide dwellings for all colonists on board, it also provided a multitude of hiding places for the Native Americans known to inhabit the New England coast. Stories of what had happened to Europeans who had arrived a few years earlier and were killed by these "Indians" were well known to all on board the *Mayflower* that morning. Also well known were the gruesome details of those killings, details that would chill the blood of even the bravest within their ranks.[1] But in spite of the life-and-death struggle that lay ahead, disputes began to break out even before the small group of settlers came ashore.

Having only arrived the day before, November 9, 1620, rumblings and mutinous words were beginning to be heard as factions among the colonists began to suddenly appear. They had been given the right from King James of England to establish a colony in an area of the New World called Virginia. However, while out at sea a storm had pushed them badly off course causing them to arrive in New England instead, Cape Cod to be exact. But there was the problem. It was an area where they had no legal right to be, let alone begin the laborious and dangerous efforts to establish their colony. Had they arrived in Virginia, the small colony that already existed there would have provided a governmental structure to guide them. But here, 500 miles north of the nearest English settlement, there was no civil authority on shore nor on the ship. Over the rumble of conflicted words being exchanged on the deck that morning, no doubt some who gathered must have gazed at the forest fence just past the shoreline. If so, they could see oak trees, with pines, junipers and sassafras. There before them was an abundance of natural wealth simply waiting to be harvested, if they could remain united.

What those on board were experiencing no ordinary Englishman could have imagined in his wildest dreams. It was absolute freedom of choice and opportunity with no government controls. The intoxication of such unexpected freedom brought confusion as the realization of their circumstances began to settle in. They had absolute freedom, as well as an incredible opportunity to build wealth, all tempered by a lingering fear of the unknown and the lack of any civil authority. That fear, mixing with hope, which coursed through the minds of those on the deck that morning would be the catalyst for the first democratic meeting ever held in America. But little did those gathered know that the very act of their meeting, and its result, would alter the course of history.

For most on board the reason for coming to the New World centered on seeking the ability to worship God in the manner of their choosing. They were escapees, in a sense, from the religious requirements placed on all Englishmen by their king to worship through the established state-religion, the Church of England. Originally, they had fled England for Holland, seeking religious freedom, but soon that "haven" began to lose its luster. It was then they initiated contact with the Virginia Company, an English company established to colonize North America for profit. The Virginia Company then secured the *Mayflower*, as well as the rights to settle in Virginia. The Virginia Company also brought other settlers along on the voyage who sought not religious freedom but wealth.[2] They were entrepreneurs, and for them the shackles of Europe against the common man bettering himself were reason enough to brave the dangers of the New World. It was here where no European aristocracy could control their every action, telling them what they could and could not do.

As the fateful meeting began that morning on the deck of a ship whose name would live forever, the voices of those that chose to speak certainly must have mixed with the sounds of nature: the gusty wind, seagulls overhead, and waves lapping against the side of the ship. And, indeed, it was an appropriate beginning, since it was nature that would have to be conquered, if they were to survive. Under such life-and-death conditions, man's mind tends to become focused, making him more reasonable and open to the ideas of others than he might otherwise be under less dire circumstances. There is no record of who spoke that morning or of what was said, but the result of their gathering was monumental. In the end, all of the men on the deck signed a self-governing agreement, creating a civil authority acknowledged by all colonists that would be the law of the land. They chose a governor, John Carver, the first freely elected in the New World. Having signed the auspicious agreement on the deck of their ship, they called it the "Mayflower Compact."[3]

Throughout the remainder of November 1620, the self-governing group sent expeditions to scout the mainland for the right place to build their colony, but with little progress. Then as December dawned, the reality of their struggle began to hit home. On December 4, Edward Thompson died. Then in rapid succession on December 6, Jasper dies; he was the servant of Governor Carver. On the 7th, Dorothy Bradford, the wife of future governor William Bradford drowned. This tragedy was immediately followed on the 8th with the death of James Chilton, while on an expedition to the mainland. During the remainder of December, two more of their original 75 died. In January and February, the harsh winter took so many more lives that by winter's end, a little more than half of those who came from England were alive.[4] Indeed, it was a difficult land.

Eventually, a location on the mainland was chosen, and housing was built there, providing a semblance of a town. They called it Plymouth Plantation. Then as spring blossomed so did the hopes of the settlers who had survived the winter. The spring planting season presented both an opportunity as well as a danger. If successful it would be an important foundation for a future with adequate food, allowing the colony to grow and eventually prosper. But if unsuccessful they would starve to death since the food brought with them on the *Mayflower* would soon run out.

However, a fateful decision had been made at the time the Mayflower Compact was signed. Governor Carver had determined the small colony would unite their efforts at farming, instead of each man striking out for his own benefit. The idea was that their collective results at farming would go into a common pool to be evenly distributed among all in the colony after the harvest. There is little doubt that those of the entrepreneur spirit must have objected to this commune-based, instead of private-enterprise based economic system. But on that day long ago in the wilderness of the New World, their voices were not heard.

According to the ancient Greek philosopher Aristotle, "That which is common to the greatest number has the least care bestowed upon it." Governor Carver should have read Aristotle. The colony nearly starved. After two years of mediocre crops and severe food shortages, resulting in severe hunger, there was a genuine fear the colony would not make it through the winter of 1623 unless something was done to dramatically increase the next harvest. Then another great democratic debate ensued pitting those in support of the collectivist system against those who embraced free enterprise. In spite of the problem of near starvation resulting from the employment of the collectivist system, there were some who wanted it to continue, believing that if employed for another planting season, the results would be different. On the other side of the debate were those who believed the results from employing the same collectivist system would remain the same, thus presenting the real possibility that the colony would starve to death during the coming winter. They promoted a free enterprise approach to food production wherein each individual was responsible for the planting and harvesting of their own food.

It was settled in 1623 when the new Governor, William Bradford, after hearing various opinions, agreed with those espousing a change to private enterprise. Bradford had noted in his diary that the commune system had "breed much confusion, and discontent, and retard much employment." He also observed how individuals "would allege weakness and inability" so as not to have to work for the benefit of others.[5] Because of the small size of the population of the colony at that time, there is little doubt everyone knew how badly the commune system was working. This makes the opposition to changing to a new system of private enterprise, on the part of some, difficult to understand, especially in light of the near starvation the colony experienced as a result of the collectivist system. Later that year as the harvest began coming in under the private enterprise system, the results were beyond the colonists wildest dreams, producing a bounty of such magnitude that any fears of starvation were now gone. The fledgling colony had been saved.

Based on the old writings, there is little doubt some groups opposed Governor Bradford's idea to relinquish government control over the economy, turning it over to a private enterprise system that would empower the individual.[6] Their opposition came in spite of the monumental failure of the old system, which not only led to near starvation, but as Bradford wrote, "breed much confusion, and discontent, and retard much employment." However, their opposition only appears difficult to understand until it is placed within the proper context. Just as the move toward private enterprise empowered the individual, at the same time it effectively disempowered the few who had controlled the old collectivist system. At the time of Bradford's decision, the colony had grown to approximately 180 persons as colonists continued to arrive from England. As such, since their numbers grew, so did the power of those few individuals who controlled the results of their labors.

There is no clear record as to exactly who opposed Bradford on the issue, but logically only two groups would suffer from such a move. Those who controlled the old system who would lose their power over the others, and those who "would allege weakness and inability," since now they would have to work.

Had there been a system in place wherein the knowledge of how badly the collectivist system had preformed could have been withheld from the colonists, the results of the debate might have been quite different. Under such a scenario, two natural allies would have existed to retain the old system: those who sought control over others and those allergic to work. In theory the only chance those two groups would have to retain the old collectivist system would have been to somehow control how the colonists viewed the cause of the reported employment chaos and its attendant near starvation of the colony. In theory, had there been a mechanism in place wherein they could have created a different reality of what had caused the hunger and employment problem, then perhaps their forces would have been able to retain control. Such an effort would have surely involved attempts to alter the perceptions of those impacted. Of course, under the close-knit conditions that existed within the small colony at that time, altering the reality of the cause of the crisis was impossible.

But the event would mark the first time in the New World that a strain of individuals seeking to control others had reared their heads, coming together in the cause of control. However, it would take a few hundred years before their ideological prodigy would finally achieve that control through the advent of technological advances.

Over the course of time as the population of America grew, the free flow of information would continue to empower the masses in every walk of life, making despotism impossible. As the years passed, it no longer was the small size of the population that enabled the people to be informed, but a network of small newspapers. Then in 1831, a Frenchman by the name Alexis de Tocqueville came to America to observe its staggering freedom, famously writing about the utter impossibility of any media within the country possessing enough power to *manipulate* the American people. And, indeed, to understand how American democracy ended in the last decades of the twentieth century, it is necessary to understand the stubborn foundation that protected the masses from those seeking to control them.

✼ ✼ ✼ ✼ ✼

He came to America to study the prison system, but upon departing would write a book viewed by many to be the most astute observation of American democracy ever written. That book, *Democracy in America*, is described as "at once the best book ever written on democracy and the best book ever written on America."[7] His writings scan the length of American government, society, intellectual movement, and a host of other topics relating to what made America free. But it is his observations of the free press at that time that strikes the deepest chord when compared with what exists in America today.

The year is 1831, and as de Tocqueville arrives in America, he sees for the first time what true freedom and democracy really look like. As a European aristocrat, he instinctively understands the controlling hierarchy of the Old World and how it suppresses the freedom of the masses within his beloved France. The French Revolution several decades earlier had not established the democracy he and many had hoped would be its result. Instead, democratic "institutions" would appear, only to disappear once again under some change in the political winds. It was only the year before his coming to America that the French monarch, Charles X, was overthrown during a revolt in Paris. The king had attempted to establish his supremacy by eliminating freedom of the press, and dissolving the freely elected Chamber.[8] His "coup" was stopped in its tracks by a polyglot of students, workers, and the lower bourgeoisie. However, the democracy de Tocqueville observed in America was completely different from what he saw in France. It was stable and possessed the self-controlling feature of deeply ingrained religious beliefs alongside social mores he observed in people of all walks of life. Such beliefs, he found, acted as a kind of invisible hand regulating the behavior of the citizens, making them suitable for running a democracy.

What a Free Press Looks Like

At the time de Tocqueville wrote *Democracy in America*, the media in America consisted wholly of newspapers; there was no radio, television, or Internet dominating the attention of the masses. As he surveyed the scene of American democracy, he noted how almost every town, regardless of its size, had its own newspaper. This compared significantly from what he had seen in France, where there was a *centralization* of control over the press, with only a few controlling its major organs. In a series of interviews he conducted with Americans he considered enlightened, de Tocqueville concluded that it was the *decentralized* nature of the press in America that represented the critical feature in support of the nation's freedom. He noted how within such a *decentralized* system no small group could control any more than a tiny portion of the distribution of information, and this resulted in a press unable to exert any influence toward a common goal. In his book he notes how there was no power center for the press, and that "news" flowed from all parts of the country, not having any press "capital" directing what was to be considered newsworthy.

> The United States has no capital: enlightenment like power is disseminated in all parts of the vast region; like rays of human intelligence, instead of starting from a common center. ...
> The Americans have placed the general direction of thought nowhere...[9]

His observation that "the general direction of thought [was] nowhere," is a clear reflection of its *decentralized* nature. In his travels to New York City, he saw no vast media complex disseminating its version of news and social mores to the rest of the nation. What he did see across the land was the incredible ease with which a newspaper could be established, and attributed the "lack of power of the press to this incredible scattering of its strength." Seeing no *centralization* of the press in the hands of the few led him to make a profound observation.

> One conceives without difficulty that among so many combatants [newspapers] neither discipline nor unity of action can

be established. ... Newspapers in the United States, therefore, cannot establish great currents of opinion that sweep away or overflow the most powerful dykes.[10]

He is deeply impressed by the complete inability of the press to combine its efforts in a common cause, wherein it "cannot establish great currents of opinion that sweep away or overflow the most powerful dykes." It is relegated to the position of reporter to the people, and thus allows democracy to function with the masses directing the nation. If one newspaper chose not to report something, others elsewhere would and thus relegate the first news outlet impotent at censorship. As de Tocqueville saw it, the essence of what constituted a free press, its *decentralized* nature, prevented any band of ideologues from colluding in order to control what the nation would think.

In addition to *decentralization* producing a truly free press, he points out another important benefit flowing from it. Since starting a newspaper was so easily done, and therefore a multitude of them existed, the profitability of each was small, if at all. This phenomenon, de Tocqueville pointed out, would keep "great industrial capabilities" from becoming involved. He recognized the danger to the free flow of information to the people if great financial interests become involved in its dissemination.[11] He clearly recognized the benefits of preventing a few corporations from controlling the better part of what the masses see and hear. What de Tocqueville is observing is a time of true democracy with the masses ruling in America.

He goes on to point out what Americans sought from their newspapers was knowledge of the facts, not the personal opinions of reporters. Then quite prophetically he warns,

only in altering or in denaturing the facts that the journalists can acquire some influence for his opinion.[12]

In other words, only when a reporter alters or withholds certain facts relating to a story can he *manipulate* the beliefs of his audience. His reasons for doing so would probably stem from either ideological or personal preferences, which he was seeking to pass on to his audience. But again, since within a *decentralized* press his audience represents only a tiny part of the masses, his *manipulative* efforts are for naught. And since the media was completely *decentralized,* the natural flow of competition among its various outlets prevented censorship from occurring. But de Tocqueville understands the dangers of how a centrally controlled press can *manipulate* the masses, having watched its machinations within France. As a result, he makes an observation that underscores the need for a completely *decentralized* press for a democracy to function.

> When a large number of organs of the press come to advance along the same track, their influence becomes almost irresistible in the long term, and public opinion, struck always from the same side, ends by yielding under their blows.[13]

His description of such an event as "blows" being delivered against the very people the press was meant to serve underscores the need for a *decentralized* press in the eyes of de Tocqueville, one not able to be controlled by any group seeking to push their will upon the masses. de Tocqueville knew the uniting of the press within a democracy would win the day for any cause it championed, given enough time. Therefore, only in the case of something happening where people across the land generally shared a common belief would there ever be a chance of a *decentralized* press uniting in a common cause. However, in that case, they would have no ability to alter the beliefs of the people, but only to confirm them.

The possibility of a *decentralized* media leading the nation politically or in social mores did not exist when America possessed a free media, which explains the long-term stability in beliefs held by Americans since Plymouth Plantation. Without any powerful force weighing upon the minds of the masses attempting to impose its will upon them, they were allowed the freedom to naturally develop their own beliefs as a society. And with such a highly *decentralized* media, both the people and the press would remain free.

However, it wasn't only a *decentralized* media that kept American democracy viable. But as observed by de Tocqueville, it was even more the religious beliefs embraced by the masses, producing social mores and morals that stubbornly refused to allow despotic forces to rise. It appears that this foundation against despotism had developed because a natural evolution in the beliefs of the masses was allowed to proceed, unhindered by any powerful force imposing its will. Since despotic individuals have existed across time, and within every civilization, such freedom was not the result of their absence. It was a result of their not being able to gain a wedge of power over the masses. And this is a great surprise to him—something he had not observed within the European countries he was so familiar with.

Religion & Political Freedom in America

Upon arriving in the United States, de Tocqueville notes "it was the religious aspect of the country that first struck my eye." His statement is impressive considering the large amount of observations he would record in his two volumes concerning America. But the difference he sees relative to religion's impact on freedom in America versus that which he knew in France is striking. After making the observation of how in Europe the lessening of religious belief appears to be in direct relationship to the increase in "their brutishness and ignorance," his observation here is that "in America one sees one of the freest and most enlightened peoples in the world eagerly fulfill all the external duties of religion."[14] As

a well-educated European man, he has seen much in his travels and studies, but not the phenomenon of enlightenment alongside deep religious
conviction. It clearly fascinates him.

But there is another factor in addition to the practicing of religion
that de Tocqueville finds absolutely essential to maintaining democracy
in America. It is found in the social mores of the people.

> ...I consider mores to be one of the greatest general causes to
> which the maintenance of a democratic republic in the United
> States can be attributed.[15]

Then he expounds further on this concept of mores.

> ...not only do I apply it to mores properly so-called, which one
> could call habits of the heart, but to the different notions that
> men possess, to various opinions that are current in their midst,
> and to the sum of ideas of which the habits of the *mind* are
> formed.[16] (Emphasis added)

To de Tocqueville the social mores of the masses are a distinguishing
factor that sustains democracy in America. So much so that after he notes
the democracy-inducing advantages of North America from a physical
standpoint, i.e., no powerful enemy on its border, he points out that the
laws serve to maintain a democratic republic more so than those physical
advantages. However, strikingly, he observes the social mores embraced
by the people appear to be even more important than the laws for maintaining democracy. He is dramatically impressed with American morals
in sustaining democracy.

The America that de Tocqueville observed was one well-suited for
democracy, which he observed was largely due to the completely *decentralized* nature of the press, allowing the people to rule instead of individuals who found a way to monopolize control over what the masses were
told. But it is also the deeply held religious convictions and social mores

of the people, acting in unison, he saw as essential in protecting freedom, creating a stubborn buffer against despotism.

As an island set apart from the Old World, it was within the New World that the masses were allowed to develop those religious beliefs and social mores without directives from any ruling political elite. As such, they developed in a way that complemented democracy, instead of countering it. So much so it was a surprise to de Tocqueville as he went about making his historical observations. This set the masses of America apart from those in Europe, creating a land ripe for freedom and leading to the greatest success story history had ever seen.

But the vast freedom de Tocqueville would witness had its foundations laid years earlier by a political philosopher who would be the guiding light of the Founding Fathers. His words would establish the justification for declaring independence from Britain and set up the foundation of democracy and true freedom of mind and spirit that would blossom across the land. But just as his political writings would establish that foundation, hundreds of years later his words would serve to identify the tyranny that has risen.

CHAPTER THREE

The Foundation

As the winds of war blew their mighty gusts, sending the American and French armies toward the coast of Virginia, it appeared that their common foe had been surprised. The first surprise for the British was when the French fleet, consisting of 24 warships, suddenly appeared at the mouth of the Chesapeake Bay, ready to confront the smaller British fleet stationed there to protect its army at nearby Yorktown. The result was the Battle of the Chesapeake, and although it was inconclusive from a military standpoint, from a strategic perspective it was a major blow to the British navy.[1] It resulted in their withdrawal from Chesapeake Bay, effectively stranding the British army at Yorktown. The second surprise for the British was the size of the force confronting them by land at Yorktown, with the combined American and French troops numbering 17,000 against a British force of only 9,700 defenders.[2] The impact of that unpleasant reality made escape by land impossible. With an exodus by sea eliminated, and outgunned almost two-to-one on land, the British army was surrounded. Suddenly, six years after the rebellion of American colonies against British tyranny had become a full-blown revolution, the possibility of a colonial victory became quite real.

Finally, on October 19, 1781, the surrounded British army at Yorktown surrendered to an aide of American General George Washington, effectively ending the war.[3] Relief, especially among the leaders of the Revolution, swept the land. Of the many prominent colonists who had supported the war effort, all had faced a terrible future in the event their treason had failed. British kings tend to take a dim view of rebellion as the long list of those who had visited the royal guillotine could testify. As such, it was nothing less than their lives that rested on the outcome of so dubious a venture as to challenge the world's mightiest army. As the reality that freedom had been won settled in, the great task of governing fell to those who had risked their lives to bring it about.

John Locke & Thomas Jefferson

In the days leading up to the signing of the Declaration of Independence, a document whose fame and impact would grow over the course of time, Thomas Jefferson remained secluded at his home working through its nuances. Already well-versed in the major political philosophers of his day, the document he produced would eventually lead to an independent nation from what had been the colonies of Britain. With the grand signature of John Hancock, it would represent the culmination of years of tension between the colonies and the British monarch. But for Jefferson, credited as author of the powerful and historical document, it was the political philosopher John Locke whose influence would greatly impact his writings, with Jefferson regarding him as one of three men he held in the highest esteem. He would include Locke in his "trinity of the three greatest men the world had ever produced."[4]

John Locke had written his *Two Treatises of Government* that people have natural rights to life, liberty, and property, which he referred to as a Law of Nature. These rights were possessed by, and fundamental to every living person, thus, they were natural rights derived by simply being born into the world. As such, he believed that the main function of government was to protect these rights, and such civil authority was limited to the specific powers given it through the consent of the people. Locke would declare that this State of Nature actually represented a condition of absolute freedom for mankind, unrestrained by the limits of a governing authority and where all people were equal.

Locke describes the Law of Nature as a Natural Law, essentially written on the hearts of men and requiring their actions toward one another to be reasonable and just. He points out that...

> The state of Nature has a law of Nature to govern it, which obliges every one, and reason, which is that law, teaches all mankind who will but consult it, that being all equal and independent, no one ought to harm another in his life, health, liberty or possessions; for all men being all the workmanship of one omnipotent and infinitely wise maker...[5]

He goes on to point out the need that "all men may be restrained from invading others' rights, and from doing hurt to one another ..." and expressing the concept "there cannot be supposed any such subordination among us that may authorize us to destroy one another, as if we were made for one another's uses." Locke's Law of Nature created a foundation for the creation of a new form of government, one dedicated to the consent of the governed, without an aristocracy of any kind imposing their will on the masses.

The impact of Locke on the political thoughts of the Founding Fathers cannot be overstated. When it comes to the Declaration of Independence, Locke's ideas would influence Jefferson to reference the "laws of nature," which maintain that "all men are created equal."[6] His famous words were paraphrasing Locke's writings that the Law of Nature "teaches all mankind who will but consult it, that being all equal and independent"[7] should respect the other. It is a novel notion begun by Locke, and then referenced by Jefferson in the document that would lead to an independent nation. The justification for such equality among men, to Locke's mind, was that all men are "the workmanship of one omnipotent and infinite maker."[8] Jefferson, on his part, would paraphrase that concept as well with the immortal words that men "are endowed by their creator with certain inalienable rights."[9] Without the influence of Locke, that phrase would have never entered the American lexicon.

In like manner, Jefferson would write other famous words derived from Locke, that the natural rights of man include "life, liberty and the pursuit of happyness."[10] But at the time they were written, none thought Jefferson invented them. Rather, the Founding Fathers knew they had come from Locke, who sees fundamental rights as including "life, liberty and property."[11] The entire premise of Locke's political philosophy took the perspective that all government exists at the pleasure of the governed and is created through common agreement among individuals, like those on the *Mayflower*, who suddenly found themselves without civil authority to guide them. According to Locke, this right to form a government belongs to the individual and exists prior to the establishment of government. Here, too, Jefferson would incorporate this concept representing a major pillar of the American political structure, stating "governments are instituted among men, deriving their just power from the consent of the governed."[12]

But it wasn't just in abstract political thought that Locke's impact was felt. He was the first to describe the practical delineation of political power into a system of checks and balances, which we know today as the separation of powers.[13] According to John Adams, such a division of power was incorporated into the United States Constitution to achieve the Lockeian goal of protecting "life, liberty and property." Why would it protect those founding goals? It was because by *decentralizing* political power into separate branches, no small group of individuals could place a tyrannical hold on the nation. So the entire concept of separate branches of government was derived from the notion that *decentralization* of power is necessary in order to maintain a democracy, because once power becomes *centralized*, tyranny becomes possible. Such a concept was completely new at the time Locke wrote those words. But having just come out from under British tyranny, the Founding Fathers incorporated Locke's concept as the central feature of the U.S. Constitution. As such, the United States government consists of the executive, judicial, and legislative branches of government. Without Locke, this may not have happened.

Locke is also the first to argue for the separation of church and state in his work titled, *Letter of Toleration*. Locke's influence can be seen in similar writings by the Founding Fathers such as James Madison in *A Memorial and Remonstrance on the Religious Rights of Man*[14] as well as Jefferson's *Act for Establishing Religious Freedom*. Eventually this concept derived from Locke would find its way into the Bill of Rights.

Locke's philosophical writings would also delve into what constituted a state of war among men, as well as slavery, conquest, and the usurpation of the rights of man. Such concepts were not just theoretical in their nature, but quite practical because he understood that the nature of certain men causes them to seek to bring others under some form of domination. Locke goes on to say the following:

> And hence it is that he who attempts to get another man into his absolute power does thereby put himself into a state of war with him; it being understood as a declaration of design upon his life ...for nobody can desire to have me in his absolute power unless it be to compel me by force to that which is against the

right of my freedom – i.e. make me a slave.[15] (Emphasis added)

They are words that moved many of the Founding Fathers, including Thomas Jefferson, against the tyranny of the British crown. He is describing basic, and for that time, relatively new tenets of the rights of man to freedom.

> The liberty of man in society is to be under no other legislative power but that established by consent in the commonwealth, nor under the domination of any will, or restraint of any law, but what that legislative shall enact according to the trust put in it.[16] (Emphasis added)

According to Locke, any force acting outside the trust of the people's legislature that attempts to impose its will over the masses is in violation of the fundamental rights of man. Such a violation would certainly include small groups of individuals possessing similar goals and such power as to enable them to exert their common will over the masses.

In his chapter "Of Conquest," Locke states that such aggressors, although they may achieve that dominion over the liberty of others, shall "never come to have a right over the conquered." He points out the general understanding among mankind that none "think robbers and pirates have a right of empire over whomsoever they have force enough to master."

Following this line of reasoning in Chapter 8, "Of Tyranny,"

> As usurpation is the exercise of power which another hath a right to, so tyranny is the exercise of power beyond right, which nobody can have a right to; and this is making use of the power anyone has in his hands, not for the good of those who are under it, but for his own private, separate advantage.[17] (Emphasis added)

Here he establishes that there is a tyranny that seeks to exercise power beyond which any can have a right. This would include power, gathered through a sudden advancement of technology, which allowed a small group to gain ascendency over others. Such powerful warnings would impress those who had risked their lives against the British crown, leading to a myriad of safeguards erected in the governing document they would devise, with Thomas Jefferson prominent among them.

The impact on Jefferson from Locke's writings would go beyond the Declaration of Independence, and would stay with him through his long life. On the 50th anniversary of its signing, Jefferson would write Roger Weighman in Washington that the signing was,

> The Signal of arousing men to burst the chains ...and to assume the blessings & security of self-government that form which we have substituted, <u>restores the free right to the unbounded exercise of reason and freedom of opinion</u>.[18] (Emphasis added)

With Jefferson having had time to deeply absorb the historic events from years earlier, he makes it clear that "the "unbounded exercise of reason and freedom of opinion" are fundamental rights, the loss of which would constitute the assemblage of chains about those so encumbered, and represent the loss of a significant freedom. This right, however, is distinguished from the myriad of physical freedoms spoken of, such as taxation without representation, and the right to assemble, but instead focuses on the minds of the people. Using the words "unbounded exercise of reason" Jefferson aligns against those who would, in some manner, encumber the ability of the masses from utilizing their reasoning abilities. There is little doubt he would not have given an exception to any who found a way through technological advances to achieve such control over others. After all, how free can a person be whose mind is not allowed the "unbounded exercise of reason?"

Not many years after Jefferson wrote those words, Alexis de Tocqueville confirmed that the "unbounded exercise of reason" existed across the vast expanse of the nation. He attributed such a state of freedom to the highly *decentralized* nature of the press (media) throughout the land, alongside strong and rigid religious convictions and social mores. Whereas the *decentralized* press in the form of countless newspapers dispersed across the land offered no despotic opportunities to alter such exercise of reason and opinion, a certain advance in technology some 120 years after de Tocqueville arrived in America would change that.

PART II

Manipulating Man

CHAPTER FOUR

The Age of Manipulation

Although the continuous explosions had become a constant reminder that time was running out, it was now the rumble of tanks closing in on the center of the city that began to create hysteria. What remained of the leadership of the thousand-year Third Reich was now gathered at the Fuhrerbunker, an underground safe haven located in the center of Berlin.[1] But with the Soviet army closing in, it came to represent the heart of a dark empire convulsing in the death throes of its last gasp for life. Due to their status within the ruling Nazi party, many of those gathered within its concrete walls had lived a privileged life in Germany during the 1930s. But with Berlin falling to angry hordes of Russian troops, that distinction now became a death warrant. As the Soviet noose tightened around the vicinity of the bunker, its more resourceful occupants began implementing secretly devised escape plans. Some would escape, but most would die or be carted off to the nether land of the Soviet gulag system, never to be heard from again.[2] The fiercest fighting took place on the streets immediately leading to the bunker, with the remaining German troops knowing they were literally defending their leader. But with overwhelming numbers, the Soviets were unstoppable, capturing the bunker and essentially taking the city at that moment. As the victorious Soviet troops began entering the smoldering compound that only hours earlier had been home to the most odious regime of modern times, they came upon a box containing tapes and various documents. The information contained within the box revealed Nazi plans to utilize television (TV) within Germany on a grand scale. The plan included programs for sports, education, and news with the goal of capturing the interest of the German people, so that ideological messages could be fed to them. Of course, every message would in some way augment Nazi control over their minds. Although it was to be designed as entertainment, it would be done for control. The key, it seems, was to get a TV into every German home. Walter Bruch, the German engineer in charge of this task, had sent the plan to Adolf Hitler for his approval and was ready to develop, as he called it, "people's television."[3] Josef Hebbels, considered the mastermind of the plan, had informed the sister of Nazi leader Rudolph Hess...

> We'll be able to show whatever we want. We'll create a reality, which the people of Germany need and can copy.[4] (Emphasis added)

What Hebbels and the Nazi leadership understood was that television could easily, and effectively, be used to shape the beliefs of the German masses, so they would conform to the will of those who controlled it. Considering the efficiency of the Nazi propaganda machine in that day, their faith in the ability of TV to accomplish this is enlightening. Hitler had already used the new technology during the 1936 Berlin Olympic Games but only with limited success since there were so few "viewing screens" throughout Germany at that time.[5]

However, by the time the bunker was overrun in 1945, the plan for every German to possess a *viewing screen* was ready to be implemented so shows of interest could weave political messages within them for mass absorption. It appeared that the new technology of television appealed to the Nazi warlords.

In short order after the war was over, other despotic characters would come to realize the benefits of television's *centralized* nature and begin using it to alter and shape the thoughts of the masses they sought to control. Joseph Stalin, the leader of the Soviet Union, whose troops had discovered the Nazi plan, used it as a prototype for his efforts at mind control within his own nation, which some years earlier he had so violently imprisoned. Then, throughout the 1950s and forward, Soviet TV would *create a reality* that many within its borders would embrace, ready to die for a false cause, but not understanding it to be one. With years of powerful images sent to *viewing screens* (TVs) within homes throughout the workers' paradise, most would believe they, and not the Americans, were economically better off. But even within the virtual slave conditions of that socialist police state, there were in existence *rogue elements* that knew the truth. As a result, a word-of-mouth "media" developed, questioning the party line. Throughout the Soviet satellite states of Eastern Europe, a similar story played out with Soviet ideologues firmly in control of the *viewing screens* (TV), able to send images and voices into the homes of the people they sought to control. A new age of *manipulation* had dawned upon the weary masses, with their masters not only seeking to control their economic production, but their thoughts as well.

Then with the blossoming of the Cold War between America and Russia, transmitting stations were erected around the peripheral states surrounding the Soviet Union, within nations that sided with the United States in that stand-off. From those stations were transmitted *rogue programming* that attempted to penetrate the ideas which had been pressed into the minds of the Soviet masses largely through the use of *viewing screens.*[6]

America

Within America, the new and powerful technology played out differently. With the entrepreneurial spirit in place since the days of Plymouth Plantation, it wasn't the government that developed television, but companies seeking profit through advertising revenue that increased as audience levels did. However, unlike newspapers that were never suited for central control, television technology, a natural for *centralization*, resulted in only three large corporations capturing the market for the entire United States. By producing programming that entertained, everyone wanted to have a *viewing screen* (TV) to receive free entertainment and news. Although in 1946 less than 1 percent of American homes had one, by 1954 it had skyrocketed to over 55 percent, and by 1962 it was almost universal.[7] Because of its *centralized* nature, the big-three corporations that controlled the transmissions coming through the *viewing screens,* were all located in the same place-New York City. With the ability to send images into the homes of the masses and tell a story, their power to control the various debates democracies experience grew beyond anything the nation had ever before known. And for the first time in American history, a few individuals controlled what the people were being told.

❈ ❈ ❈ ❈ ❈

At his most primal level, man seeks to control his fellow man. There is little need for proof of this truism, as it is observable at every level of life. Some attempts take place within individual relationships, others the family circle, some at work, and also within a political structure. Some attempts are blatant, some brutal, but others are subtle and only take their

toll over the course of time. It is this subtle type that is the more insidious and difficult to see. True control forces others to do something they
would not do if left to their own will. With the exception of children,
usually when someone needs to force another to do something, it is because the case in favor of doing so is weak. As a result, wherever there is
a free media for the masses to gather information, unhindered by *manipulation* and censorship, individuals trying to control others are usually frustrated. The group of colonists in the year 1623 who tried to convince Governor Bradford to retain the old collectivist system was unable
to convince their fellow colonists. They were unable to *create a reality*
to overcome the one embedded in the colonists' minds from the experiences of near starvation resulting from that system. But none-the-less,
that result did not stop those that had controlled the old system from
attempting to retain control over the economic production of the masses.
Once tasted, power becomes addictive.[8, 9]

As the power of television continued to grow within America, naturally so did the interest of political ideologues in controlling it, and for
obvious reasons. The power to send images into the homes of the masses
and *create a reality* on a *viewing screen* had previously never been available
in the history of mankind. This presented a political ideologue's dream
come true. With no law in place to ensure the new technology's complete *decentralization*, and thus democratization, it became vulnerable.
It is reasonable to think that had the Founding Fathers, who so carefully
erected myriad safeguards against tyranny, understood what the future
of communication technology held, they would have surely erected one
here as well. But without such knowledge of the future, the democracy
they had risked so much to establish saw its first threat.

Like those in Bradford's day who wanted to retain control over the
productive capacity of the colonists, that strain of individual who strives
to control the economic results of the masses, also naturally gravitates to-

ward the control of information. But since America from its earliest days benefited from a *decentralized* press, there was no chance of any group of individuals controlling what the masses saw and heard. As a result of that *decentralized* press, those who espoused the virtues of more government economic control, as well as greater control over the lives of the free, were not successful. They could not convince the masses that their vision for the nation was superior to what was in existence.

※　※　※　※　※

The first signs of an ideology becoming dominant within the television industry occurred in the 1960s with the prosecution of the Vietnam War, where the television media would occasionally be accused of giving aid to the enemy.[10] Years later, under the Freedom of Information Act, released FBI files revealed that trusted evening news TV anchor, Walter Cronkite, had assisted anti-war protesters in staging an event so it could become "news."[11] During the time he was doing that, it appears nobody within the ranks of that network took issue with his actions. The purpose for pointing this out is not to debate the wisdom of that war. But since his action was viewed across the entire nation, it is to observe a phenomenon that could not exist under a *decentralized* free press. Had control over the *viewing screens* been *decentralized* from its beginning, Cronkite's efforts would have only impacted a tiny sliver of the population, as would any attempts to *create reality*. This is because collusion within a *decentralized* media, as observed by de Tocqueville, was impossible. It was impossible because it was *decentralized* and thus, free.

A few years later in 1968, with the election of ideological conservative Richard Nixon to the presidency, friction between his administration and the television networks reached such a point that his Vice President, Spiro Agnew, was assigned the task of outing them for their ideological agenda.[12] Later in his presidency when a political spying scandal was uncovered, involving elements of Nixon's reelection campaign, TV would repay the unwelcomed exposure of its ideology with unrelenting coverage of the scandal to the detriment of almost all other stories, until Nixon finally resigned from office.[13] Although Nixon had not been the first president to be involved in a scandal, he became the first to resign, bringing many to the conclusion that it was the *viewing screens* that had accomplished it. This is not to justify a former president, but to acknowledge the role of the *viewing screens* in his being driven from office.

But that would only be the beginning of complaints against television falling under the control of an ideology. By the end of the century, there would be a litany of serious books documenting the ideological thrust of television within the United States.[14] However, by that time the observation of de Tocqueville, that the free press in America had no ability to come together in a common ideological cause, had been turned completely on its head. And there is little doubt the Frenchman would have instantly recognized how this had happened; its most powerful organ had become *centralized*.

❈ ❈ ❈ ❈ ❈

As the power of the *viewing screens* began to penetrate the minds of the masses, things began to change in America. One of the first changes showed up in their spending/saving habits. Since the earliest days, Americans possessed a strong tendency to avoid significant amounts of indebtedness.[15] This national trait started in the 1600s with the first colonists and continued into the twentieth century, providing financial stability for countless families over the years. However, by the latter half of that century, with *viewing screens* now in every home, powerful images with convincing messages resulted in Americans turning over their money for consumer goods soon to be stored away in the closet, having little use to them. In fact, from the 1920s until the mid-1950s, consumer debt had only inched higher from year to year. But beginning in the late 1950s, with the sudden mass promotion of products on *viewing screens,* it began skyrocketing off the charts and continued its dizzying pace higher from that time forward.[16] It was one of the first demonstrations of the incredible power that those controlling the *viewing screens* possessed over the minds and behavior of the masses, since money is held so closely to the heart. So successful were those who designed these images with their messages sent into homes, that the masses went from being great savers to some of the most indebted people in the world.[17, 18]

Being able to alter such ingrained national behavior within a matter of decades is, indeed, a testimony to the power of those who control the *viewing screen* content. As such, an entire industry developed with individuals dedicated to designing messages to shape and mold the beliefs of those staring into their *viewing screen.* Psychological studies on how to alter beliefs and control the behavior of the masses became a sub-industry.[19] However, with the masses repeatedly being told they must possess an object they are assured will bring them either happiness or status, over a period of time their credit cards were run to the limit. But it was not only within the financial realm where the power of the *viewing screens* to command thoughts and thus the behavior of the masses were felt.

It is apparent that those who sought to control and direct others had paid attention to the advent of television technology, finally seeing an opportunity to bring a convincing understanding of their ideology to the masses. As individuals embracing this *ideology of control* realized the power of the new medium to press beliefs into the minds of the masses, they began entering the new industry in droves.[20, 21, 22, 23, 24, 25, 26] Since those who embraced the *ideology of control* had seen their ideas rejected since the 1600s, the opportunity must have been exciting. Programming designed to alter long-held American moral beliefs began being introduced, slowly at first, but over a period of time took their toll on the social mores of the masses. The programming was designed to subtly begin whittling away at long-held moral restraints, a little at a time, so as not to incur a backlash. The moral beliefs attacked by this *ideology of control* were ones that had been a staple of American beliefs since as early as anyone could remember, handed down by the ancestors of almost all families over the course of centuries. But by showing very appealing types of individuals on the *viewing screen* engaging in certain moral acts, the historically embraced teachings of the masses against such behavior began to erode. As such since the beginning of these re-education efforts on the part of the *ideology of control* using the *viewing screens*, the vital statistics of the nation began to take a noticeable turn for the worst in every category.

Additionally, as the art of programming became more convincing and influential, it was discovered that it possessed the power to tell the masses what to wear, how to speak, how "smart" people think, and how to act.[27] However, the *ideology of control's* greatest accomplishment has come in the area of morals and social mores. Considering that Americans had essentially held the same foundational moral beliefs since the time of Plymouth Plantation, handing them down from one generation to the next, altering such ingrained beliefs is no small task.[28] But with the ability to enter the homes of the masses and tell a story on a *viewing screen,* in a relatively short time span, the acceptability of moral concepts that had been anathema since the time of the first colonists, soon became established.

Control of such a powerful medium within the hands of the few has seen its effects in the political realm, as well, where there appears to be no ability to deal with a host of serious problems confronting the nation. The reason for this is that the political process has been retarded by the effects of replacing a *decentralized* free press with that of a *centralized* one operated by individuals embracing an *ideology of control.* Any effort made to resolve a problem that crosses their ideology comes under assault from the powerful *viewing screens.*

MANIPULATING MAN

But the effort to replace the morals and social mores of the masses was not the only area those embracing the *ideology of control* would exercise with their new-found power. As the ideological prodigy of those in the day of Governor Bradford who had sought to retain the old collectivist system, they favor government control over economic production and distribution. Using the powerful *viewing screens,* they promote an increased government role in the economy, often to the point of determining who receives benefits and who does not. These efforts for control have resulted in the creation of myriad "programs" designed, ostensibly, to help the masses, but with the ultimate effect of creating dependencies that hinder individuals in supporting themselves. In addition to the creation of the economically dependent, this *new economic order* allows many of those newly dependent to be directed politically toward leaders who embrace the *ideology of control.* This is because dependents on government payments have a strong incentive to see a larger and more controlling government.

Part of the effort to establish greater government control over the economy is by *creating reality* that those politicians who embrace it are more compassionate toward their fellow man than those who embrace free enterprise. But a study conducted in 2006 found the opposite to be true. The results indicated that those opposed to greater government control over the economy contributed a higher percentage of their incomes to charity than those embracing more control.[29] When it came to who donated more of their time to philanthropic activities, as well as their blood, to the sick, again, the same results were found. It also found that one of the most pro-free enterprise presidents in modern times, Ronald Reagan, donated a higher percentage of his income to charity then two stalwarts of greater government control, Franklin D. Roosevelt and Ted Kennedy.[30] Additionally, famed economics professor Milton Friedman would establish that during the height of free market capitalism in the

19th century, an unprecedented rise in philanthropy was experienced.[31]

By consistently promoting politicians who support this *new economic order,* there has been established a significant number of individuals capable of working who have become dependent on some form of government payments. This *new economic order* is designed to attract such people into it who "allege weakness and inability," that they might join the ranks of the *ideology of control.* Although a benevolent society extends help to those truly in need, the *ideology of control* seeks to extend benefits well beyond those truly in need for the purposes of control. This is because after being brought into this *new economic order,* many are easy to direct toward politicians who support its expansion. In line with that reasoning, when a president who strongly supports the *ideology of control* is in office, there should be great efforts made to expand the government. A good example of this occurred under the administration of President Barack Obama. Succeeding in shifting the massive health care sector of the economy to government control, he also heavily advertised the availability of food stamps during his first term. As a result, the ranks of those dependent on them rose from 30 million under the previous administration to 47 million by the end of his first four years in office.[32] This great shift toward more government flows naturally from those embracing the *ideology of control* upon attaining power.

But the entire effort goes beyond just physical dependency in the form of checks in the mail and extends into the psychological. This is accomplished by the *created reality* that those receiving such government payments are somehow entitled to them, in spite of many never having contributed financially to sustain the system. Such an example is seen in the large government-run Social Security program where workers who pay into the system have a reasonable expectation of a future return on that investment. However, those embracing the *ideology of control* have utilized this system to expand the awarding of payments to masses of individuals who "allege weakness and inability," on the basis that they too are entitled to them. This observation is easily confirmable by how many people receive such payments who are visibly capable of working, as opposed to those where it is equally obvious who really need help. But with a natural drive to expand government wired into those seeking control, benefits have been extended to large numbers of the able-bodied "disabled," drawing out the funds that workers contributed into the system for their retirement. After being granted the status of "disabled," many can be directed to support political leaders who sustain this *new economic order*.

The entire system represents the coming together, once again, of the same two groups of individuals in the day of Governor Bradford, who sought to retain the old collectivist system. They were those who sought control over the production of others, and those who "allege weakness and inability." Just as in the day of Bradford, these two groups are natural allies and unite in common cause, with one seeking control, and the other a free ride. In addition to those who "allege weakness and inability," there are others who have effectively joined the *ideology of control*, those who fill the ranks of the ever growing government apparatus.

Since the *ideology of control* sees greater government as an end in itself because it creates more control, those working within it are handsomely rewarded, often far beyond what a similar position within free enterprise would have economically justified. This subtly *creates the reality* that the government is superior to free enterprise; after all, it pays much better. It also creates a mechanism of alliance between the *ideology of control* and those working within government. How this happens is quite simple. The government workers come together in a united effort to "negotiate" with political leaders for ever-increasing pay and benefits. In turn, the political leaders who agree to these terms then receive the votes and cash contributions from these same worker groups. This system is one of self-perpetuation and results in a circle of mutual support.[33]

Because governments naturally seek expansion and greater control, this threat was historically counter-balanced by an array of forces in place since America's beginnings. There was a natural balance that served the cause of freedom and democracy, and presented an impenetrable barrier to tyranny. However, with the advent of *viewing screens* controlled by an ideology possessing a need to control the masses, that calculus changed. Being the result of the *great dichotomy*, it was unable to be factored in when the nation was born and has given rise to a new and illegitimate power within the land.

CHAPTER FIVE

The Dark Empire

As the rhythmic sound of rain striking the large windows of the conference room appeared to be increasing, in the distance, the rumble of thunder could be heard joining it in a symphony of nature. Located on the 44th floor of one of New York City's best-known skyscrapers, the room was perfectly placed to view the expanse of the city's evening lights. But tonight those lights were viewed through sheets of rain that had the effect of creating beautiful distortions of their countless points, causing them to dance on the window panes in harmony with each successive wave from the heavens. Through it all in the distance, the silhouette of a giant figure could barely be distinguished in the night sky, the vague light emitted from its torch giving away its position, eventually allowing the entire figure to come into focus through the dark weather. Just as the meeting was about to begin, a flicker of lightning in the distance could be seen, indicating the worst was yet to come.

This evening's gathering was no ordinary meeting, but included some of the television network's top executives, as well as executives from the Hollywood company that would be producing a new mini-series for their upcoming prime-time season. The network had viewed itself as a pioneer in taking America into the twenty-first century, exposing it to ideas contained within its entertainment programming it hoped would open minds. With a large segment of the population tuned-in day and night, the ability to present new and challenging ideas to the masses was quite real.

As the discussions began, the main topic focused on just how far the new series should go in challenging a certain traditional moral belief relating to marriage, without pushing too far. The whole process was a kind of art in motion, knowing the tipping point of what would produce too-strong a negative reaction and then bring the message just up to it without reaching it. Some in the room had actually won awards for their skill in such efforts, although the award was titled much less provocatively. By reaching that goal, it usually accomplished two basic achievements. The first was to bring profitable controversy to the new show. After the initial flap simmered down, people tended to tune in to find out what the scrum was all about. That represented the profit motive. The second was the social benefits achieved. In this case a new understanding of marriage could be introduced to the masses, many of whom continued to stubbornly cling to a more traditional belief in the ancient institution.

But that's where frustration set in for those in the room. Many in the conference room on that stormy evening had always found that it was necessary to beat around the bush a little when introducing a new moral belief to the masses. If they didn't, then the blowback could be great as centuries of ingrained beliefs were directly challenged. This meant they had to go slower in introducing the masses to certain ideas much slower, in fact, than many in the room felt was fair. The frustration was especially strong due to the myriad important messages still needing to be delivered. As such, many in the room viewed their careers as much more than just another job, but rather a sacred trust, a ministry, in a strange way, to witness a new and better way of thinking to the masses.

As the fury of the wind and rain engulfing the conference room grew, what had been the rumble of thunder in the distance now became a booming light show just outside the windows. But as if to emphasize the importance of the discussions being held, the occupants of the room, strangely, continued as though nothing was happening on the other side of the thin glass separating them from the torrent of elements.

Everyone in the room knew that if the new show was successful, it would probably become an award-winning career-maker, bringing accolades from across the television industry and Hollywood for having pressed a new set of advanced morals into the minds of the masses. Of course, none of the awards would actually say that. The discussion then turned to just how the new social belief would be introduced through the *viewing screens* to the masses. In fact, everyone in the room already knew how it would be accomplished, since they had seen it done many times before, and it always worked. Well, it always worked for most people staring into their *viewing screens*. There were always the stubborn, and those viewed as extremist, who did not go along. Everyone in the conference room knew that those types would always be there. However, dealing with them was easy, and, in fact, necessary. They would be marginalized, isolated as backwards, and even presented as dangerous. This was necessary because if not dealt with properly and timely, those *rogue elements* could begin impacting the intellectual growth of others who were willing to learn.

The beginning phase for planting the new moral belief was really quite simple. It was all about *creating a reality* for the masses staring into their *viewing screens*. The star of the show is to be presented in a highly favorable light, very ethical, smart, good-looking, kind, etc. Then after establishing this character in the minds of the masses, the star will reveal a belief in or a tendency to practice this new moral belief system. The next step is the introduction of individuals who resist the new belief system. They will be presented in the most negative light possible, subtlety, of course. First, it is necessary to ...

Has the above narrative played out within the offices of America's *centrally controlled* television? The anecdotal evidence supporting that versions of it has is both observable and strong. There are certain trends since the 1950s within television that are observable, and have cut hard against the morals of the vast majority of people in the nation, essentially promoting a new set of beliefs that had been rejected by the masses since the first colonists arrived on the shores of North America.[1] One such trend has been the litany of counter-traditional moral messages that have been woven into programming transmitted through the *viewing screens* with growing intensity. Essentially, the messages transmitted are ones that are embraced by only a tiny minority at first, until after a period of continuous repetition, more and more of the masses begin to embrace it. Often, such messages were designed to replace traditional moral concepts with ones that had been anathema to the vast majority since America's earliest days. Not only has that phenomenon been observable, but also the clear trend toward ever-increasing extremes of those messages. As such, it appears there is an ultimate goal designed to replace the traditional moral order of beliefs that stood since the time of the first settlers until the 1950s, with some kind of a *new moral order*.[2, 3, 4]

With *centrally controlled viewing screens* able to project images and sound within the homes of the masses, and thus possessing immeasurable influence over their minds, it would be reasonable to conclude that if they were directed toward replacing one set of moral beliefs with another, then results would surely follow within society. And that observation is the easiest of all to make. Since the time *centrally controlled viewing screens* began promoting this *new moral order*, a dramatic shift in the moral belief systems embraced by the masses has been seen. It is observable that within that time frame traditional moral beliefs have been replaced with beliefs unrecognizable to any previous generation of Americans. It can also be observed that there has been a clear direction to it all, indicating a powerful force behind this dramatic shift away from what previously had been the ingrained moral beliefs of the masses. If there was no new and awesomely powerful force injected into society capable of accomplishing such a shift, then it would not be happening.

Since the basic moral belief systems of Americans had not changed in any substantial way until the 1950s, it essentially rested where it had since the 1600s.[5, 6, 7] That is not to say that natural adjustments to it had not taken place, but to say no kind of watershed shift had occurred within that time frame. And since there was no force powerful enough to move the moral beliefs of the entire nation in a new direction, it appeared that basic morals would remain where they had always rested. Most would agree that moving the morals and social mores of a nation is a Herculean task, to say the least, with such ingrained beliefs representing a substantial object at rest and resisting significant movement.[8] According to Newton's First Law of Motion, something at rest remains at rest unless disturbed. As a foundational law of physics, in line with that reasoning, something at rest will suddenly begin moving only if an "unbalanced force" begins to impact it.[9] It is the *viewing screens* in the hands of ideologues that became that unbalanced force, powerful enough to disturb the place where the morals and social mores of the masses had rested since the early 1600s.

In years past, any group espousing a new moral concept was limited to introducing it to only a small fraction of the masses due to the *decentralized* nature of media that existed in America. This makes sense since decentralization divides power, effectively disabling those seeking to alter beliefs on a massive scale. As a result, any attempt by individuals to introduce a *new moral order* was confined to a small area and had to run a gauntlet of *natural checks and balances* represented by the accumulated body of judgments of each individual within society. And therein, no powerful force existed that pressed them toward acceptance. Such judgments were formed by upbringing, family, and traditions. Therefore, the introduction of any new moral concept had to go through a process of societal approval that took time, allowing for the careful consideration of what was being proposed. Since there was no *centrally controlled* media, and thus a free press existed, collusion was impossible, and any new morals could be introduced only within a confined area. As de Tocqueville would point out, since the press was completely *decentralized,* there was no ability of collective efforts by the media to promote a cause. The acceptance or rejection of a new moral concept was completely determined by individuals and only within the very limited proximity of its initial dissemination.

Therefore, what flowed from this truly free press was the most basic of human rights: the right of the masses to evolve their own set of moral beliefs. If one part of the country began to accept a new moral concept, other areas would hear about it only if the fervency of the first in embracing it was great enough. Otherwise, because of the decentralized nature of the media, it would tend to remain peculiar to that area alone. But if embraced with fervency, then the chances of other regions being exposed to it would grow in a natural way, allowing those other areas to pass judgment on its worthiness, accepting or rejecting it, representing yet another *natural check and balance.* Over the course of time, a moral concept that made it through such a series of *natural checks and balances* would only then become embraced by the nation. This system of *natural checks and balances* flourished under a *decentralized* media, allowing the masses to decide their own set of moral beliefs, and representing freedom of choice instead of the *imposition of choice through overwhelming influence.* So the masses were able to exercise the "unbounded exercise of reason" and "freedom of opinion" heralded by Jefferson as so critical to the exercise of freedom in general, the loss of which represented the assumption of chains about the people. But with the advent of *centrally controlled viewing screens,* all of that changed.

One might argue that the dramatic and historical shift toward embracing this *new moral order* has happened because of the superiority of the new beliefs contained within it. But that argument does not hold up under scrutiny, even after ignoring the immorality of using technology to alter beliefs on a mass scale. Since Plymouth Plantation, until the advent of *viewing screens*, fundamental moral beliefs remained basically unchanged, except for certain relatively minor changes that passed the *natural checks and balances* of the masses over the course of time. In fact, those long-standing morals appeared to work well for America during the four centuries that they lasted, with a variety of social measures testifying to the collective wisdom of the people in embracing them. They resulted in a cohesive family unit, a low crime rate, a strong savings rate, and a good work ethic. Additionally, there was no significant illegal drug use, teenage pregnancy, nor, for that matter, rampant venereal disease. The *natural checks and balances* of societal morals worked.

But since the 1950s as *viewing screens* began appearing within every dwelling across the land, the most dramatic shift in fundamental moral beliefs in world history rapidly began taking place.[10, 11, 12] As the new beliefs being pressed began taking hold within the minds of the masses staring into their *viewing screens*, all vital statistics for the nation began plunging. The family unit, to a significant degree, was destroyed. Individual debt skyrocketed just as savings plunged. Crime became a terrifying fact of life with countless lives lost to its growing and unstoppable rampage. Illegal drug addiction brought misery to countless lives. Additionally, the American people have been successfully divided into groups, one pitted against another with one favored and another disfavored on *viewing screens*.

This sudden and dramatic change in fundamental social beliefs co-incides with the spreading of *viewing screens* across the nation and their transmitting messages that introduced a *new moral order*. Once again, based on simple logic, it tells us that some new and obviously very pow-erful influence, an unbalanced force, has been injected into the body of the nation, one capable of dramatically influencing beliefs. Otherwise, the historically sudden change in fundamental moral beliefs could never have occurred naturally. Considering the countless billions of dollars spent by corporate America to transmit messages through the *viewing screens* with the express intent of altering and directing beliefs, and thus behavior, what more needs to be said?[13]

❖   ❖   ❖   ❖

With new morals having been successfully planted within the minds of the masses using carefully designed messages transmitted through their *viewing screens*, the credit for the content of those messages goes to the entity known as "Hollywood." Although the term Hollywood denotes a physical location within the state of California, it also identifies a center of control where the production of those messages takes place. Like its sisters, the television networks, its nature is ripe for *centralization* and thus control by common ideologues. In fact, the single city name given it denotes its *centralized* nature.

No doubt that possessing the power to alter the beliefs of the masses has to be an intoxicating one. But over the course of time, such power tends to corrupt, impacting the judgment of those possessing it occasion-ally causing words to be spoken which later are regretted. In his book, *Primetime Propaganda*, Ben Shapiro interviewed several powerful Hol-lywood moguls who went too far on video, unable later to pull back their careless words. Whatever the reason for their brazen words, what they had to say was as revealing as it was anti-democratic.

Producer Susan Harris, of *Soap* and *Golden Girls* fame would proudly proclaim to Shapiro concerning the political activism of Hollywood, "At least you know, we put Obama in office, and so people, I think, are getting have gotten a little bit smarter."[14] Essentially, she was bragging about utilizing *viewing screen* entertainment to direct the masses to support a politician, President Barack Obama, well known for favoring increased government control as well as the *new moral order*. She would also discuss hiring practices within Hollywood, making it clear that those who embraced traditional beliefs need not apply. Under a *decentralized* media, such efforts to *manipulate* the masses would never get through the *natural checks and balances* that stood in the way, allowing the masses to remain free to develop their beliefs without the *imposition of choice through overwhelming influence*. Such a use of technology to shape and mold the beliefs of the masses appears to represent the assumption of chains warned of by Thomas Jefferson, resulting in the loss of the "unbounded exercise of reason and freedom of opinion."

Hollywood executives Larry Gelbart and Gene Reynolds talked about certain messages woven within various long-running shows, such as the hit series *M*A*S*H**.[15] Producer Vin DiBona, creator of several shows including *America's Funniest Home Videos*, stressed that anti-gun rights messages were woven into his shows. When asked about traditional-thinking Americans missing from the ranks of Hollywood, DiBona would emphatically respond, "I think it's probably accurate, and I am happy about it." Leonard Goldberg, executive producer of numerous shows over the course of decades, pointed out that "liberalism in the TV industry is 100% dominant, and anyone who denies it is kidding, or not telling the truth."[16] Liberalism, of course, promotes ever-greater government control as well as the *new moral order*. Fred Pierce, former president of ABC television network in the 1980s, was clear about the importance of proper hiring within Hollywood, indicating that when it comes to the dominant ideology within Hollywood, those who don't lean left "don't promote it. It stays underground."[17] Again, those on the left side of the political spectrum are identified partly by their enthusiasm toward the *new moral order,* as well as greater government control. Unwittingly, Pierce, indirectly, acknowledged that unless the *new moral order* is promoted, "it will stay underground" and will not be able to replace traditional moral beliefs. This mindset also explains why those embracing the *ideology of control* were attracted to the *viewing screen* industry in the first place, because unless they can *impose choice through overwhelming influence,* their beliefs stay underground. And they *impose choice through overwhelming influence* by the constant drum beat of *created reality* pressed into the minds of those staring into their *viewing screens.*

But the most vulnerable in society to this *created reality* are the young, and for the most obvious reason. Since they have limited life experience to draw upon in comparing the present with the past, they lack a depth of reference, and thus many are not yet well enough equipped to identify *manipulation.* As such, they are assured by those seeking to mold their minds that such malleable beliefs, as embodied by the *new moral order,* make them superior to their ancestors. And it is this ability to *manipulate* the minds of the young that produced more excitement than one Hollywood executive could emotionally handle, speaking words not able to be found in the previous histories of North America. MTV Networks Entertainment Group president, Doug Herzog, even more direct than others in his industry, bragged about possessing "superpowers" over the <u>minds</u> of young people[18] (emphasis added). Herzog and those who work for him are masters in weaving a combination of *viewing screen* images with music to implant the *new moral order* within the minds of the young, using the process of repetition of message.

Such "superpowers" would have immediately been recognized by Jefferson as well as John Locke. It was Locke who warned that slavery is established when an individual is placed "under the domination of any will" other than that established by the consent of the people. Certainly, the masses have never knowingly granted such "superpowers" to any in the land.

Nicholas Meyer, producer of *The Day After*, which depicted America the day after a nuclear war, was broadcast on ABC during the Reagan Administration's efforts to negotiate a nuclear treaty with the Soviet Union. When asked if people who embraced traditional American values were discriminated against in Hollywood, he retorted, "Well I hope so." Then Meyer would add, "*My private*, grandiose notion was that this movie would unseat Ronald Reagan when he ran for re-election"[19] (emphasis added).

John Locke would have clearly related to Meyer as the kind of man he warned about in his chapter titled, "Of Tyranny." Therein he identified those types of actions as "the exercise of power beyond right, which nobody can have a right to... but for his own *private, separate advantage*." (Emphasis added) Under a *decentralized* media, such types could never rise to a place of power over the minds of the masses, since they would have to pass through the *natural checks and balances* of a *decentralized* media. Such *natural checks and balances* protected the masses against those seeking to place chains that "encumber the unbounded exercise of reason and freedom of opinion." With many more interviews of the same kind, the author of the book eventually concluded "Most nepotism in Hollywood isn't familial, it's ideological."[20]

The impact of such "superpowers" has been studied by science and psychiatry, producing results that reinforce how much power *viewing screens* have over the minds of the masses. In 2002, *New Scientist* magazine reported on the results of a 25-year study of violent shows produced by Hollywood. The findings concluded that "TV watching increases the risk of violence by five times," indicating a depth of influence over the minds of the masses, which directly translated into aberrant behavior.[21] This conclusion had already factored out other circumstances that tend to contribute to violent behavior, rendering no effective criticism of the results. Since man's earliest days it has been the dream of tyrants to possess such "superpowers." But in this case the tyrant is not a single individual, but a collective of common ideologues.

In March 2011, the American Academy of Child & Adolescent Psychiatry revealed that the effects on children are even more destructive. After acknowledging television as a powerful influence in developing "value systems" (i.e., *new moral order*) in children, it observed that the violence seen by children during their *viewing screen* sessions caused them to "imitate the violence they observe."[22] Besides the cost in innocent human life, a price is also paid by the culture, shifting it away from the tradition of benevolence and toward one of self-destruction. By spreading such destruction across society, there is no doubt that ideologically driven *viewing screens* have accounted for the tears of many grieving families over the course of their existence.

The question raised by all of this is not if these persons have a right to promote their beliefs. Even despotic individuals have such a right. Rather, it is that within a *decentralized*, and thus free media environment, their influence would be no more than that of the common man, who within America was doing just fine prior to their ascension. However, within a *centralized* media, the moral beliefs of those that control it are being passed on to the masses, pressed into their minds through constant repetition that no democracy can account for. The right to impose their beliefs on the masses does not appear to be a result of any election by free-minded persons understanding the entitlement being granted. Instead, it appears to have resulted simply by the fact that an *ideological collective* managed to gain control of the powerful *viewing screens.* This type of influence, never granted by the people, represents what Locke and Jefferson feared most.

In order to justify the exercise of "superpowers" over the minds of those staring into their *viewing screens,* one must believe those so engaged have a right to do so. However, that "right" is nowhere to be found in Natural Law as described by Locke, nor within the U.S. Constitution. Effectively, in utilizing their near monopoly over the *viewing screens,* this *ideological collective* has successfully placed the masses "under the dominion of [another] will ... for [their] own private, separate advantage." As such, their actions constitute the enslavement of those vulnerable to their methods.

※   ※   ※   ※   ※

If it is true that an *ideological collective* controls what the people see and hear, and its power to plant a *new moral order* into the minds of the masses, there should be other observable traits within its realm as well. And, indeed, there are. For those who own and control the television networks, as well as the Hollywood production facilities, they possess the power to bestow fame on those they choose to, essentially creating famous people out of virtual nobodies. Therefore, if a specific ideology is in control, then we should see a large majority of those who they choose to make famous falling in line with their *new moral order.* This, too, is observable. It is observable that a vast array of actors and actresses stand on the side of the *new moral order,* promoting it where they can, with those in opposition almost invisible. To prove this truism, simply consider how few of those made famous by the *viewing screens* have taken a position against the *new moral order.* Within an industry where hiring was based on talent, and not ideology, this phenomenon could not occur.

If it is true that the nature of television technology lends itself to control by the few, then there should arise another observable phenomenon, that of increasing *centralization* of control. In the time de Toc-queville wrote, there existed countless media outlets (newspapers) dis-seminating information to the masses with no ability to combine their efforts toward any cause. With the advent of television technology and the ability of a few to *centrally control* it, that has dramatically changed. By 1983, the number of corporations that controlled a majority of media in the United States, including television, was a scant fifty. By 1990, the number of such corporations dropped to just twenty-three. By 1992, that number declined to only fourteen, and by 1997, ten. The observation by de Tocqueville that a completely *decentralized* media (newspapers) in America allowed democracy to flourish, in hindsight is obvious. How-ever, by 2004, control over almost all of what the masses saw and heard was consolidated into the hands of only six companies.[23] As this increas-ing *centralization* has occurred, coincidentally, so has the acceleration in the promotion of the *new moral order*.

Those six corporations are the following: General Electric, Time Warner, Walt Disney Corp, News Corp, CBS Corp, and Viacom. Not only do they control all major television networks (ABC, NBC, CBS, FOX, and CNN) but also almost all cable networks including MSN-BC, CNBC, History Channel, A&E, Biography Channel, Bravo, USA Network, SyFi, Oxygen, Chiller, Hallmark Channel, Sundance Channel, Telemundo, HBO, Cinemax, Cartoon Network, TNT, TBS, Turner Classic Movies, CW, Time Warner Cable, ABC Family, ESPN, Disney Channel, Lifetime, Hulu, Fox Movie Channel, FX, National Geograph-ic, Fox Sports, Showtime, Movie Channel, MTV, Nickelodeon, Spike, VH1, BET, CMT, Comedy Central, Logo, and Vira. With such a deep reach, they control almost everything seen on the *viewing screens*. But that isn't where their control stops.[24]

Within Hollywood they control most major production facilities such as Universal Television, Universal Studios, Warner Brothers, New

Line Cinema, Castle Rock Entertainment, Hanna Barbera, Touchstone, Miramax, Marvel Studios, 20th Century Fox, CBS Television Studios, Paramount Studios, and United International Pictures.[25] Such a monopolistic system of controlling both production and distribution has, throughout American history, been considered contrary to the basic tenets of freedom.

Via the Internet their *centrally controlled* reach extends even deeper with an audience of over 95 million unique visitors each month to websites of just the top three, CBS, MSNBC, and ABC.[26] CBS is the leading supplier of videos to Google, whose reach is immense. And don't think that "social media" is countering that Internet dominance. The overwhelming majority of individuals accessing "news" from mobile devices, for example, seek to access known names for their "news" sources, not the recommendations of friends on Twitter and Facebook steering them to *rogue* sources. Therefore, these six monoliths are beginning to add to their control over what the masses see and hear, using the Internet.[27] As a result, the information that counters the *created reality* of the *new moral order* is seldom seen, with those taking a stand against it dwarfed by an overwhelming array of media.

All told the combined media holdings of these six corporations reach more than 1,050 significant individual media outlets. They include all major TV networks, Cable networks, local TV stations, cinema and TV production facilities, almost all of the big-name magazines, many of the big-name newspapers, a multitude of significant Internet sites, and publishing houses responsible for the vast majority of books published. As a result, the media holdings of these six monoliths account for over 90% of everything the masses see and hear.[28] But the crown jewels are their *viewing screen* holdings, wherein the ability to move the masses in virtually any social and political direction is found, and having proven capable of accomplishing the task in very little time.

MANIPULATING MAN

The Five Forces of Order within America

There exist five compelling *forces of order* within America that bring domestic tranquility, prosperity, and freedom, and have existed since the first colonists landed at Cape Cod. They are the family, the church, culture, free enterprise, and the government. The greatest freedom exists within the first four, and, thus, they represent a *force of freedom*. The fifth, government, can augment freedom by protecting minorities from oppression, ensuring that monopolies do not develop, provide for the common defense against foreign invasion, and, in a more general sense, simply remove obstacles out of the way of the first four. A *decentralized*, and thus truly free press, causes the *forces of freedom* to prosper since such a media has no ability to direct and control what the masses think. With the uncontrolled free flow of information from a *decentralized* media, it is the masses who direct the nation, as observed by de Tocqueville in the day when a free press flourished. However, a *centrally controlled* media, especially as it relates to the *viewing screens* because of the great influence they exert over the mind, is a friend of the government simply because it diminishes the flow of information to the *forces of freedom*.

Whenever the family, church, culture and free enterprise are strong, they do not allow the government to grow in power, and as a result freedom prospers. During such periods when the *forces of freedom* dominate, government is allowed to gain power only during times of war or great economic calamity. But because there is a continuous battle between the *forces of freedom* and government, after a crisis is over, wherein the government was granted greater power to deal with some great issue, the *forces of freedom* attempt to retrieve the additional power it gave. Likewise, after such an event, the government attempts to retain that newly granted power. This is why those who embrace the *ideology of control* view any crisis as an opportunity to expand control. It is also why the manufacturing of a crisis by those seeking control is always a possibility.

During periods where the *forces of freedom* are strong, individuals who embrace the ideology that seeks to control others are frustrated in their efforts. This i*deology of control* always pushes for greater government power because government, by its nature, is a force for control. As such, the enemy's list, if you will, of the *ideology of control* are a strong family, a vibrant church, a cohesive culture, and a free economic system, essentially the *forces of freedom*. In order for the i*deology of control* to achieve its goal of control, it must lessen the influence of the *forces of freedom*. Like those in the day of Governor Bradford, certain individuals have a strong desire to control the production of others. In the Plymouth Plantation case, the effort revolved around controlling crop production and its distribution. But their effort to retain control failed. Since that time, until the advent of *viewing screens*, it had been essentially the same story for those embracing the *ideology of control*. As the former television network executive stated, unless their ideology is hired, "it stays underground." America didn't hire them, nor were they able to impose themselves.

The main reason for their inability to enact control over those centuries was because they could not *create a reality* over a widespread area, or convincing enough, for the masses to see things their way. However, with the advent of *viewing screens* erected within the homes of the masses, an opportunity was presented for their *ideological collective* to *create a reality*, finally allowing it to exert influence over the belief systems of the masses.

Having taken control over what is transmitted through the powerful *viewing screens*, the *ideology of control* then set out to attack the *forces of freedom,* in order to weaken them since they naturally oppose greater control. That is why the *ideology of control* is always pressing its *new moral order,* as well as greater government control, over economic production because both undermine the *forces of freedom*. Additionally, since the government and the *ideology of control* are natural allies, both always support increased government regulations and authority. That, too, weakens the *force of freedom.*

This explains why since the 1960s the *ideology of control* has used the *viewing screens* to *create a reality* to promote a *new moral order* and a *new economic order* that undermine the family, religion, free enterprise, and culture. By so doing, it has weakened the *forces of freedom* standing between it and total control of the masses. It has done all of this in the shadows. With the advent of *centrally controlled* communication technology developed within the twentieth century, allowing a small band of ideologues to control what the masses see, and hear, and with the power to replace belief systems with their own, the *ideology of control* has succeeded in becoming an unnatural sixth *force of order* within America. Being unnatural and possessing a desire to avoid the light of exposure, it operates from within a realm of darkness, always ready to deny that it is engaged in *manipulation* of the masses. With its tentacles now reaching into the minds of most within the land, it has evolved into a *Dark Empire,* altering the balance of power between the *forces of freedom* and the government.

Some may find that the term *Dark Empire* appears to be too dramatic in describing this *ideological collective* that controls the *viewing screens.* But for those who do, here is something to consider. The pages of history are filled with groups of individuals, in different places and at various times, who came together for the cause of controlling the masses. When it is done for the imposition of private goals, it is their own actions which place them on its darker pages. And the fact that the masses were entertained into it does not lessen the blow.

But such a despotic entity as this *Dark Empire* took time to evolve into what it has become. Although its evolution is a natural tendency of those embracing the *ideology of control*, its method of evolution was anathema to the notions of freedom and democracy.

CHAPTER SIX

Ideological Cleansing

T wo years before the Nazi juggernaut drove fire and steel into the breadbasket of the Soviet Union, the leaders of both re-gimes had signed a pact of friendship and peace, much to the surprise and consternation of the nations around them.[1] It was a cyni-cal agreement between the world's worst dictators, effectively granting Hitler a free hand to invade whomever he chose, and he would choose quickly. Within the agreement there existed a secret codicil whereby the two leaders determined the fate of the brave Poles, whose nation was planted between them and that would soon be violently divided, each dictator getting a part. What Stalin gained from the deal was the buffer zone of Poland, as well as the false hope that the Nazi madman would satisfy his craving for "living space" somewhere other than the Soviet Union. But that was not to be. Having established a perfect record of violating the agreements he made, Hitler would soon turn his guns on his partner in "peace."[2]

MANIPULATING MAN

The German invasion, code-named Operation Barbarossa, began on June 22, 1941, and would become a life-and-death struggle for both nations, with Hitler eventually losing his gamble.[3] But in spite of that great drama unfolding, one that would determine the fate of the world, the two combatants continued to purge their nations of individual citizens who did not agree with their ideology. One would have thought that with such a great struggle taking place, they would have focused all energies toward victory. But their fear of internal dissent appeared to be too great. This type of *ideological cleansing* had been going on since the founding of both governments, with each establishing a system for dealing with their fellow countrymen who dissented. In Germany, the system included the infamous Konzentrationslager, or concentration camps, which found their counterpart in the Soviet Gulag system. More than simple jails for various types of prisoners, they represented the foundation of an effort to cleanse society of all who did not embrace their new order.[4, 5]

Common to dictatorial systems is the fear that an open discussion of issues will hinder its ability to effectively *create reality* for the masses. As such, they must continuously cleanse their ranks of any that may not fall in line with the new order being presented. With the advent of mass communication technology in the twentieth century, allowing the whole country to see and hear the same thing at the same time, a powerful new tool for controlling the masses appeared on the world stage, one that every oppressive regime would embrace. This power to *create a reality* on a mass scale enabled others without the use of guns to attain control over the masses as well, presenting their own *new order,* which encompasses the *new moral order* as well as the *new economic order.* Those others would evolve within nations that are typically described as "democracies." But since that term implies rule by the masses, it is better to describe them as nations that hold elections. However, in order to attain that control, they first had to cleanse their ranks of those who did not fall in line. Otherwise the message being presented would become blurred, losing much of its effectiveness. And that is where our story of this *Dark Empire* picks up.

❈ ❈ ❈ ❈ ❈

There are some who would grant a pass to those seeking to control the masses so long as guns are not employed to accomplish it. But that assumes freedom is something for the taking and without support within the Law of Nature. Morally speaking, no one possesses the right to take such freedom from another, no matter how ingenious the method used. As Thomas Jefferson would point out many years after writing the Declaration of Independence...

> The Signal of arousing men to burst the chains ... and to assume the blessings & security of self-government that form which we have substituted, <u>restores the free right to the unbounded exercise of reason and freedom of opinion</u>. (Emphasis added)[6]

Indeed, it is the "right to the unbounded exercise of reason and freedom of opinion" where this *Dark Empire* has run afoul, employing the *great dichotomy* of powerful technology to the detriment of both rights. It is especially its homogeneous nature, wherein there appears to hardly ever be a noticeable breach within its ideologically purified ranks, with seldom any *rogue message* slipping out that challenges the *created reality* of its *new moral order* being presented. From centralized portals, its very nature lends itself to the gravitation and domination by a single ideology. This is because it lacks the freedom-inducing influence of *decentralization*. As such, there has developed within its ranks a natural system of self-perpetuation that appears to continue playing out, granting it longevity.

MANIPULATING MAN

Natural Selection

Political ideologues have a tendency to assign intelligence and other favorable attributes to those who share their beliefs. This natural form of gravitation tends to confirm what each has been thinking and creates a bond among fellow believers. It also tends to feed upon itself in certain other ways. One is the development of a system in hiring that represents a form of *natural selection,* creating, and then perpetuating an ideologically pure system. This is done through the natural tendency of political ideologues to advance those who ideologically agree with them. That is to say there is a tendency for a political ideologue to hire a common political ideologue, who, when his turn comes, hires another common political ideologue and so forth. This form of *natural selection* is very simple and its implementation in the hiring process is not difficult to follow. In fact, within a system whereby ideology is viewed as important, it all happens with a natural flow.

Natural selection appears to explain the hiring process of a number of universities where faculty members who do not embrace the *new moral order,* or the *new economic order,* have all but disappeared. A poll taken in 2000 using the two major political parties as benchmarks indicated the degree to which this has occurred. Of the two major political parties within the United States, the Democratic Party clearly trends toward the promotion of the *new moral order,* as well as greater government control, over the lives of the masses. Therefore it attracts those who embrace the *ideology of control.* The Republican Party, generally speaking, opposes greater government control as well as the implementation of the *new moral order* and, thus, moves in the opposite direction. With such a clear distinction between the two parties, they can be used as reference points in identifying support for the *ideology of control,* versus opposition to it.

In the 2000 U.S. presidential election, professors from liberal arts and social sciences faculties across the nation were polled to record the breakdown of support given to the opposing candidates in that race. The results showed that almost all polled, 84 percent, supported the Democratic candidate with only 9 percent voting for the Republican.[7] However, the actual national election results that year were split evenly between the two parties. Therefore, the poll represented a result so completely out of line with the sentiments of the population as a whole, as to indicate the existence of some process within the nation's university system that has caused this anomaly to appear.

Supporting this thesis was a landmark survey conducted in 2005. Daniel Klein, Department of Economics at George Mason University, and Charlotta Stern, Institute for Social Research, Stockholm University, looked at the ideological composition of 1,678 academic professors from universities across the country. The survey titled, "Professors and their politics: The policy views of Social Scientists," showed that from the 1960s until the 2000s, based on party affiliation, "the findings indicates that during that era, the Democratic preponderance has roughly doubled" within academia across the United States.[8] The study also noted that among those Democratic professors, "the data show almost no diversity of opinion ... when it comes to the regulatory, redistributive state: they like it." As the study would also indicate concerning diversity of opinion, "Democrats show much less diversity than the Republicans." Essentially, it showed that what has evolved within the nation's universities is an *ideological collective* that is intolerant of nonconforming political views.[9] It is this "regulatory, redistributive state" that is the essence of the *new economic order*, one wherein unending regulations are used to enact control over the masses. The "redistributive state" is the coming together of the same old crew from Governor Bradford's day, those seeking to survive off the productiveness of others, and those who control them. The study's observation of a lack of diversity of opinion is a reflection of what a *closed ideological system* will typically experience, one where a diversity of views is unacceptable. And since the narrowness of opinion appears to be intensifying, as well as the preponderance of common ideologues by almost doubling, this *ideological collective* that has evolved appears to be one that has entered the *extremist spiral* of growing intensity.

Since those embracing the *ideology of control* gravitate toward control, they are the opposite of those who gravitate toward freedom. Those who place freedom as most important, by the nature of that belief system, will not seek to control through some form of cleansing process, resulting in the natural evolution of a diversity of beliefs as indirectly confirmed by the Klein-Stern study. But for those who embrace the *ideology of control*, being the opposite of those embracing freedom, they place control above freedom, causing them to naturally seek to cleanse systems so they can be brought within control. In their case the need to control trumps all else, causing their tendency toward the application of a form of *ideological cleansing,* over the course of years, where those not conforming to their belief system need not apply for a position. All that is required for the process to begin is for a true believer to rise to the top position within a university. Such an achievement represents a watershed moment for the institution resulting in, over the course of years, its ceasing to be a diverse ideological system. Such a system should eventually enter the *extremist spiral,* as indirectly indicated in the study was happening, with the *ideological collective* reaching greater and greater levels of purity of opinion and preponderance.

As a result of the successful application of *ideological cleansing* within a number of "higher education" institutions, there is now a form of unanimity within academia in the promotion of the *new order,* which encompasses the *new moral order* and the *new economic order.* Out of the top-50 universities within the nation, the percentage of professors embracing the *new moral order* and the *new economic order* represent an overwhelming majority.[10, 11]

Also within the Klein-Stern survey, the votes for president were tallied among the professors and confirmed what other studies had found. Although over the course of decades as the population of the nation was fairly evenly split between Democrats and Republicans, academia became a virtual one-party state. When votes cast for the Democratic candidate for the presidency versus those for the Republican were studied, the evidence overwhelmingly indicated that some form of *cleansing* of their ranks had been occurring. Depending on the discipline looked at, ratios such as 9 to 1, 5 to 1, and 21 to 1 in favor of the Democratic candidate were recorded, and represented results impossible to achieve unless a form of *ideological cleansing* has been taking place.[12]

In another study by Gary Tobin and Aryeh Weinberg, titled "A Profile of American College Faculty," their results provide a strong hint as to the mechanics of the process of *ideological cleansing,* but without calling it that. After noting how across the nation university faculty moved to the left during the 1960s and 1970s, they point out that it remained there ever since. Then this from the report:

> Some academic disciplines, especially the social sciences and humanities, exhibit particularly consistent political behaviors. Recruitment, hiring, and tenure review process have either failed to adequately prevent this political imbalance or have actively perpetuated and deepened political unity. (Emphasis added)[13]

It should be noted that those considered on the "left" side of the political spectrum strongly embrace greater government control over the lives of the masses and overwhelmingly support the implementation of the *new moral order.* The above quote from the study appears to shed light on the process of *ideological cleansing* that has been at work within academia, bringing it to the brink of becoming a one-party system. But all of this demonstrates something else worth noting. What has happened to universities across America flows naturally from those embracing this *ideology of control*, as control leads to a direct reduction in freedom. This reduction of freedom is reflected in the lessening of ideological diversity, which is necessary for greater control, just as increasing diversity of beliefs leads to less control. For those seeking control over the masses, the choice is clear. And what their *ideological collective* has accomplished within that system should be expected to be replicated wherever those embracing the *ideology of control* reach a level of power. It is also noteworthy within the Tobin-Weinberg study that the left-turn in academia took place in the 1960s and 1970s, which coincides perfectly with when the *ideology of control* began overtly using the *viewing screens* to press their views on the masses.

Since such cleansing comes naturally to those who embrace the *ideology of control*, if the above statements were not true then, once again, it would not be so overwhelmingly indicated by various studies, as well as easily confirmed by the simple observation. Just consider how many institutions are overwhelmingly dominated by professors who now embrace the *new moral order*. If the implementation of this *new moral order* was resulting in dramatic leaps forward for society, then the case might be made that such a dramatic ideological domination is the result of its success, thus causing it to draw all comers to embrace it. But, in fact, the opposite has occurred.

Its implementation coincides with a visible, across-the-board, societal breakdown with much grief, death, and destruction attendant to it. Compared to the condition of the masses before its imposition, it can justly be called the most devastating invasion North America has experienced. Since it is apparent that some form of *ideological cleansing* has been occurring in spite of its destructive results, this indicates its implementation is nothing more than the work of tyranny. Such a conclusion works well within the understanding that there is a concerted effort to destroy the four *forces of order* that are the *force of freedom* within America: the family, religion, free enterprise, and the culture. And all of it, ultimately, is being done in the cause of control.

But as prevalent as *ideological cleansing* is within the universities of the nation, it is within the industry of the *viewing screens* where it appears to have found almost complete success, with the exception of the news department of one *rogue element*. When it comes to the *Dark Empire,* and its control of the *viewing screens*, possessing the power to *create reality* has resulted in bold efforts to ensure its ranks remain dominated with those who embrace the *new moral order*. And their success in this regard infers the existence of a system that prevents hiring those who oppose its implementation. No other conclusion is better able to explain their almost unanimity of support for the *new moral order* within their ranks. This unanimity represents a result that is impossible to achieve unless ideology is the main consideration in the hiring process.

In a survey conducted in 1981 by S. Robert Lichter, then with George Washington University, and Stanley Rothman of Smith College, 240 journalists at the most influential national media outlets, including all major television networks, were polled on their political attitudes and voting patterns. The findings support the concept that those who control the *viewing screens* have *ideologically cleansed* their ranks of nonbelievers. When in 1964 the Democrat for president, Lyndon Johnson, won in a national landslide, the media elite recorded a 94 percent vote his way. However, in 1972 when Richard Nixon won nationally in a similar landslide, only 19 percent supported Nixon. Votes for president by media elite in 1976 went 81 percent for the Democrat as well.[14]

Every profession has its top positions that can be reached, a lofty position of respect, with significantly more income. Within network news one such position is "White House correspondent." Nowhere on Earth is more news made and of the most significant nature than the White

House. One would hope that within a great democracy those entrusted to report to the masses from so important a place would be hired on the basis of ability, not ideology. But that doesn't appear to be the case. In 1995, Kenneth Walsh, a reporter for *U.S. News & World Report*, polled 28 of his fellow White House correspondents which included all major television networks. Between 1976 and 1992, the results of the survey recorded 50 votes for Democratic candidates for president, compared with only seven for Republicans. Further breaking down the results, in 1984 10 voted for Democrat Walter Mondale and zero for Republican Ronald Reagan. However, Reagan went on to win big among the electorate. In 1988 12 voted for Democrat Michael Dukakis and one for Republican George H.W. Bush.[15] Such results reflect an industry where some form of *ideological cleansing* has been at play.

Within this *closed ideological system* the effects of *ideological cleansing* have also been observed by those working on the inside, with some occasionally speaking out. Newsweek Washington Bureau Chief Evan Thomas, speaking on one of the Sunday political talk shows, pointed out ...

> About 85 percent of the reporters that cover the White House vote Democratic, they have for a long time. There is a, particularly at the networks, at the lower levels, among the editors and the so-called infrastructure, there is a liberal bias.[16]

Andy Rooney would joke about it on the CBS show, *60 Minutes*, during the 2004 presidential election that the media was evenly divided, saying that "Half of them liked Senator Kerry (Democrat); the other half hated President Bush (Republican)."[17] In that same race Newsweek's Evan Thomas, on the show *Inside Washington*, considering the impact ideologically purified media would have on that presidential race offered, "that's going to be worth maybe 15 points" for the Democratic candidate.[18] Chris Matthews, of MSNBC fame, would reveal his observations concerning *viewing screen* purity in an on-air exchange with *Newsweek* Editor Jon Meacham, during the 2004 Democratic Convention. After Meacham pointed out that the Republican Party believed the media was all against them, Matthews would come in agreement with that sentiment stating, "Well they're right about *The New York Times*, and they may be right about all of us."[19] In an amusing exchange on CNN, after one Bill Hammer questioned liberalism's dominance in the media, Jack Cafferty asked him if he was "just off of a vegetable truck in South Bronx? They're everywhere...What do they call this joint? The Clinton News Network? (CNN)"[20] The "Clinton" referred to in this case was President Clinton, a Democrat.

CBS reporter Bernard Goldberg, while still employed with that *central controller* of *viewing screens*, would explain the natural flow of it all, stating, "No, we don't sit around in dark corners and plan strategies on how we're going to slant news. We don't have to. It comes naturally to most reporters." It comes naturally because their ranks have experienced the effects of *ideological cleansing*. Goldberg would later move on to FOX News, a *rogue element*, and become a sharp critic of what he had observed.[21] ABC "reporter" Carol Simpson, in discussing the subject of directing the minds of the masses, would state on CNBC's *Equal Time*, "I think people kind of really want you to help direct their thinking on some issues."[22] Her fellow "reporter" at NBC, Andrea Mitchell, would acknowledge when it comes to the concept of global warming stories, "Clearly the networks have made that decision now, where you'd have to call it advocacy."[23] *Boston Globe* "reporter" Dianne Dumanoski, perhaps vying for a job at one of the *central controllers* of *viewing screens*, would, unabashedly state, "I've become even more crafty about finding the voices to say the things I think are true. That's my subversive mission."[21] But in reality, what she is subverting is the "right to the unbounded exercise of reason and freedom of opinion" for the masses. Not to be outdone,

MANIPULATING MAN

Barbara Pyle, "reporter" for CNN, made it clear that "I have an axe to grind ... I want to be a little subversive person in television."[24] And within the profession of psychology some would observe this manipulation of the masses and dare to write about it. But by so doing, such individuals ensure they will never be chosen as an expert with their names, voices, and images never to be gloriously broadcast across the *viewing screens*.

In an article titled, "Media Manipulation of the Masses: How the Media Psychologically Manipulates," Dr. Samuel Lopez De Victoria, a psychotherapist and also adjunct psychology professor at Miami Dade College, observed a litany of methods practiced by mass media for controlling the masses. His observations would include the "stacking of experts" to grant the appearance of credibility while promoting a conclusion: the use of "ridicule and labeling" against those not favored in order to "freeze, isolate, and polarize that person" and the use of "repetition makes true," enabled by concentrated media power controlling what the masses see and hear on a constant basis. In his conclusion, he would urge the masses "to avoid coming to hasty conclusions just because the 'expert' says it."[25] And then, tellingly, he provided this observation.

> I don't claim to have covered all aspects of the art of deceit as used in the media. These are as old as man himself. I simply attempted to provide some of the more obvious typical forms of deceit used to psychologically manipulate the masses. What can we learn from this? Perhaps the biggest lesson could be that we must not be naïve."[26]

However, it is the nature of science to not just observe such phenomenon, but to explain it. And explanations would appear to come from other studies that look at the impact that great power over others has on the individual who attains it. Certainly, the power to shape the beliefs of the masses represents great power. One such study looked at how great power over others is capable of morphing a passive person into a dictator. The most profound and famous of those studies, "The Stanford Prison Experiment," conducted by Psychology Professor Phillip Zimbardo, looked at such an effect. In this study, now considered a classic, a group of young college student volunteers were rounded up by the Palo Alto police department and dropped off at a new jail located in the Stanford Psychology Department. They were strip-searched, sprayed for lice, and locked up with chains around their ankles. Then it was the turn of the "prison guards" to enter the scene. They were also college student volunteers. However, these volunteers were given authority to dictate 24-hour-a-day rules to the "prisoners," and it wasn't long before the power to control others began to radically alter the "guards" personalities and ethics.[27]

Soon the "guards" began humiliating the "prisoners," with Zimbardo noting how quite suddenly "the role dominated the individual." As the study progressed and the transformation of the "guards" grew darker by the day, Zimbardo decided to abruptly stop the experiment after only six days. The reason given was concern for the "prisoners." After it was over, he observed the incredible transformation such controlling power had on the "guards," noting that when the experiment began, "These guys were all peaceniks." But in the short time it lasted, "They became Nazis." He would go on to sum up the shocking results stating that, "It shows how easy it is for good people to become perpetrators of evil."[28] It is interesting to note that such "peaceniks" are typically from the left side of the political spectrum, which places them squarely in the camp of those who embrace the *ideology of control*.

Other notable studies would also record the impact on individuals attaining controlling power over others. Dacher Keltner, Ph.D, University of California, Berkley, in his study published in 2010 in the journal *Psychological Science,* would conclude "power just makes you more impulsive and self-serving and inappropriate in how you behave."[29] Ohio State

MANIPULATING MAN

University Psychologist Richard Petty would find his research suggesting that power gives people confidence in the beliefs they already possess. Noting in a *Live Science* interview that, "Power magnifies whatever is in your head. We think it kind of explains why powerful people do more good and do more bad."[30] Perhaps, such studies shed a scientific light on how *ideological cleansing* has taken place within the all-powerful *centrally controlled viewing screens*. Perhaps, once the power to influence the beliefs of the masses is tasted, a change takes place, magnifying the individual's inward controlling tendencies. In a *decentralized* media, no such corrupting power exists.

✺   ✺   ✺   ✺   ✺

Since there has been such a strong ideological thrust across the *viewing screens,* this thrust can only occur if there are too few individuals within their ranks willing to challenge it. That indicates the lack of any significant presence of *rogue elements* holding positions of importance, able to act as a natural ideological counterweight. As a result, there is another phenomenon resulting from the establishment of this *closed ideological system.* Since there exists within its ranks little or no counterbalancing ideological force, such as traditional thinking people, which are the majority of those who exist naturally within society, there is either an insignificant or no ideological counterweight present within their organizations. Therefore, there is an ever-increasing drive toward ideological extremism as each ideologue seeks to outdo the other, and thus appear to be the more advanced thinker.

Within a decentralized media, such individual efforts to guide minds would have no real impact, because they would be heard and seen by only a tiny sliver of the masses. Also, under an open system whereby hiring was not done on the basis of ideology, the mix of beliefs within that decentralized media would generally represent that of society as a whole, resulting in a healthy system of checks and balances against the dominance of an ideology and the growth of extremism. To think otherwise one has to embrace the notion that those who have been excluded because their beliefs do not conform to the *new moral order,* have no desire to hold a high position within the *viewing screens* industry. But since those Americans have been purged from the *Dark Empire's* ranks, that *closed ideological system* continues to move toward ever-greater extremes, which cause it to become caught up within its own *extremist spiral.* And this causes the *new moral order* to always move farther and farther away from traditional social mores and morals.

In order to identify extremism, one must be able to compare it to something stable. This is especially necessary in a society where ever-greater moral extremes are being introduced in rapid succession. And this can only happen if a powerful, unbalanced force is injected into their minds. Under such conditions, it is a mistake to compare only the latest advance in the *new moral order* to the advance which came just prior to it, which itself had only been introduced a short time earlier. The *Dark Empire* seeks this as a comparison in order to *create reality* that the latest new moral being presented is not extreme but only a small step. As such, the only true basis for determining extremism is to consider what existed as foundational moral beliefs and social mores until about the 1940s, before the *new moral order* began being imposed. This was the time before the *viewing screens* appeared. Only in this way can a true comparison be made.

This pushing toward ever-increasing extremes within the ranks of the *Dark Empire* has produced another phenomenon experienced by the masses, that of *continuous shock.* As the ranks of the *Dark Empire* continue their natural evolution toward increasing radicalization, due to being a *closed ideological system*, the new extreme morals they press have the effect of shocking some within the masses. This shock effect is limited to those who resist the *Dark Empire* and thus represent a more accurate reflection of how extreme the latest "advance" really is. Typically, these individuals are part of the *force of freedom*. However, the response of those whose minds the *Dark Empire* has gained ascendency over will be quite different, ranging between passive acceptance to enthusiastic embracement of the new moral being pressed.

What accelerates some to accept the new morals being pressed is the *created reality* that by embracing it they are both intelligent and advanced. In the age when the masses determined what they would embrace in terms of morals and social mores through a *natural system of checks and balances*, *continuous shock* rarely happened. This is because the masses were not under any powerful technological influence *centrally controlled* by ideologues and experienced "the free right to the unbounded exercise of reason and freedom of opinion."

There also exists the method of *institutional absorption* as the *ideological of control* drives to establish their *new moral order*. That is to say it is better to take over a moral/social institution than to develop a new one from scratch. That is because long-standing institutions have attached to them moral legitimacy. When this happens, there is associated with the process much conflict similar to what one would expect from any invasion. Those who resist the absorption of the institution will experience the wrath of the *viewing screens* across the land, *creating a reality* about them that is highly negative. These negatives usually *create reality* through the imposition of harsh *labels*. On the other hand, those pressing to absorb the institution are presented in the most favorable light, typically as kind, peaceful, full of love and understanding, and representing the wave of advanced thinking that continues to move society forward.[31] An example of this is the move to incorporate same-sex couples within the ancient institution of marriage.

The need on the part of those pressing the *new moral order* to take over institutions instead of establishing their own is because establishing new moral institutions takes centuries for their legitimacy to develop in the eyes of the masses and thus hinders its imposition.[32, 33] Therefore, by simply absorbing one that is already established, the process is accelerated dramatically. Additionally, by moving against an institution embraced by the *force of freedom,* they weaken it by taking from it a source of its sustenance. Confirming the truthfulness of this is the easily observable nature of such clashes between the *ideology of control* and *the force of freedom* centered on *institutional absorption.*

❀ ❀ ❀ ❀ ❀

Having purified their ranks over the course of decades, the *Dark Empire* has pressed its aggressive agenda of control by utilizing a particular tactic of *manipulation* that was first used in ancient times. This tactic has allowed it to reward those politicians who embrace the *ideology of control,* while punishing those who do not. Such a tactic, although disastrous for any democracy, is effective.

CHAPTER SEVEN

Divide and Conquer

He is king, but just barely. Having ascended to the throne of Macedonia after the death of his brother, who had only recently succeeded their father, he finds his rule challenged on multiple fronts. The military occupation of northwestern Macedonia by the enemy who just killed his brother and 4,000 of his finest troops is like a dagger aimed at his royal heart. But that is only where his troubles begin. Within Macedonia, there is severe turmoil with pretenders to his throne supported by foreign powers constantly nipping at his heels. And he is young, only 21 years of age, which emboldens his foes. His neighbors, the Greeks, Thracians, and Illyrians continuously attack his frontier, seeking to take advantage of what they perceive as his vulnerable condition.[1] As Philip II surveys the landscape of his kingdom in 356 B.C., he knows he does not possess the power to overcome his enemies through brute force. It is impossible; there are too many of them to confront simultaneously. But he is as cunning as a lion, a trait he will pass on to his future son, Alexander, whose name historians are destined to follow with the word "Great."[2]

The first step he takes is to shower the king of the Thracians with expensive gifts, eventually persuading him to put to death the pretender that found safe haven within that kingdom. But there is another pretender to his throne to deal with, and he is supported by the powerful Athenians and possesses his own army. Philip decides to meet him in battle and defeats him with the use of a new form of technology for warfare, one that greatly enhances the ability of his soldiers. But he has risked the wrath of the powerful Athenians for this bold act and thus a war he is not yet ready to fight. However, before Athens can react to the destruction of their puppet, Philip offers them something they crave, ceding the city of Amphipolis on the Macedonian coast in return for a treaty with them. It works. Then it is the turn of the Illyrians, who had killed his brother along with the 4,000 and still possess north-west Macedonia. But their army is strong and their position secure. However, Philip has his new technology for making war, the sarissa, or very long spear. Utilized within the phalanx formation, it is a breakthrough in the art of warfare and becomes unstoppable, resulting in the total defeat of this enemy and freeing his province from their grip.[3]

Taking less than a year, Philip succeeds in reversing his fortunes and securing his throne. He has accomplished it through the utilization of two elements of power: a new technology granting him military ascendency and a political process which history will associate with his name, *divide and conquer*.[4] His ingenious method of dealing with multiple enemies stronger than himself would be remembered by others across the march of time, bringing conquest and power to those who would master it. But it is the advance in technology that altered the balance of power that previously existed, which allowed his tactic of *divide and conquer* to be implemented. Considering these two elements of power, we now continue looking at the *Dark Empire* and the essence of *manipulation*.

Divisions

It is the technology of the *viewing screens* that has allowed the *Dark Empire* to impose its *new moral order* and *new economic order* over the masses. But America has had a vibrant history of unity in the face of challengers to its freedom, with people in all walks of life coming together in common cause throughout its history. Therefore, it was necessary to create divisions within the masses, essentially implementing their own version of Philip's *divide and conquer* weakening America and thus eliminating a united response against its efforts.

In order to achieve divisions, the masses have been systematically pitted against one another, divided into groups on the basis of sex, race, ethnicity, acceptance of the *new moral order,* and along lines of resentment, or class divisions as well as generational. By creating divisions along the lines of class, the *ideology of control* gains the added benefit of harming one of the *forces of freedom*, free enterprise. Because free enterprise is so effective in creating wealth, and therefore independent and free individuals, by causing some to resent such success, free enterprise is stigmatized.

Dividing the nation makes control easier because after a nation is divided into groups, individuals within a group tend to view their particular grouping as paramount. Many begin thinking in terms of what is best for the group, not necessarily the nation as a whole. Once that happens, it represents a watershed moment of division that finally allows many within that group to be *manipulated*.

At that point, many within the group begin to see the group's interests as most significant and then become easy to peel off in a political direction. Once this is accomplished, it allows the power of the *viewing screens* to come into play, utilized to direct the more controllable individuals within the group toward the camp of politicians who embrace the *ideology of control*. Usually the method involves driving into the minds of a particular group, through repetition of message, that they are victims or that something unfair is happening to them that certain political leaders will remedy. Likewise, it affords the opportunity to convince them that certain politicians are at war against them, trying to destroy them. Because of the ability of the *viewing screens* to *create reality*, many within these groups fall prey to this method.

Most efforts at division have been subtle, but some quite blatant. The more subtle method employed is to selectively interview individuals of the most divisive nature within the various groups, establishing them as spokespersons for that group. As spokespersons, the multitudes within that group begin to listen to them, especially around election time. The evidence of this is observed in how so many of those presented as "leaders" of a group rarely seek a broad national interest, but speak in terms of some perceived interest of their group. This is readily seen by simply observing the views of those the *Dark Empire* has made spokesmen for a particular group. Another trait of those chosen is that they almost always want some kind of special treatment for their group which, by its nature, divides.

Once a group is established, those within it are continuously reminded of the correct way to think. Since emotional loyalty toward the group is attached to this thinking, the members within the group who do not fall in line are stigmatized as disloyal to their race, sex, ethnicity, class, or even to the *new moral order*. Those individuals who bring this understanding to the group are divisive because the *Dark Empire* chose them as leaders. This is accomplished by providing them *viewing screen* prominence over an extended period of time, and thus implanting their names, faces, and voices within the minds of individuals within their respective group. Therefore, there is often a direct relationship between the amount of *viewing screen* time allocated and the divisiveness of the group "leader."

Occasionally a leader from a group rises to prominence who was not brought there through the lavishing of large amounts of *viewing screen* attention on him. If that individual does not embrace the "correct" way of thinking, then they are presenting a narrative that substantially differs from what the "leaders" of that group are presenting. This constitutes a threat to the *creation of reality* that could confuse the message being sent to the masses. Against such individuals there is an almost reflexive reaction by the *Dark Empire*. In such an event there appears to immediately begin a process of establishing a negative *created reality* about such *rogue individuals* before they can become a role model for that group. This observation was confirmed when a female politician received the nomination for vice president of the United States from one of the major political parties in the 2008 U.S. presidential election. Because she did not embrace the *new moral order* or the *new economic order* and became a highly visible role model for women, there was a stampede to discredit her across the entire spectrum of the *Dark Empire*.[5] That candidate, Governor Sarah Palin, received treatment that appeared specifically designed to discredit her among women. A study by the University of Wisconsin-Madison, published in the journal *Politics and Policy* would cite how most stories concerning her focused on her appearance, family, and social issues. However, coverage of her opponent, Vice President Joseph Biden, would focus on issues of strong interest to women such as health care and education. The study noted not only the difference in coverage but its impact. Then this ...

> If future research finds similar differences in coverage in other races, the implications could significantly affect the election process, particularly for female candidates.[6]

But that criticism was actually mild compared to a litany of others.[7, 8, 9, 10] Many observers of that race concluded that the media engaged in a concerted effort to discredit her, which begs the question, why? And the answer is quite simple. Palin was a vocal opponent of the *new moral order*, placing traditional family values at the forefront of her political life. In addition, she was also an opponent of the *new economic order*, believing in less government and more personal responsibility. Having wrapped her political career in such traditional views, the response of the *Dark Empire* against her was preordained the moment she was selected for the prominent position, representing an effort to prevent her from becoming a role model for her gender.

Since it is vastly easier to *manipulate* individuals divided into groups than it is a people united, it is critical to the cause of control that individuals within these groups maintain their group mentality. One key to sustaining such divisions is to never allow old wounds to heal. This is done through continuous reminders about past wrongs constantly sent through the *viewing screens*. In the event that old wounds within a group would heal then, over the course of time, members of that group would begin to fully assimilate into society. Should that happen, it would effectively end the group mentality and, therefore, remove a segment of society from being controllable. Such healthy assimilation, if allowed to take place, would create a united nation enhancing the pursuit of life, liberty, and happiness for all, especially those who came out of the group mentality. But it would also create a nation unable to be controlled.

Additionally, any opportunity to portray a current situation as an injustice is employed. In association with those efforts, certain information that reflects negatively on members of a controllable group is withheld from the *viewing screens*. Should such balanced information be allowed to be seen by the masses, it would begin to negate the *created reality* that the group is being victimized. This explains the drumbeat of information directed toward certain groups that accentuates the belief that they are constant victims, with seldom any indication that their group members engage in similar actions. It also explains the editing process, wherein information has been altered in order to sustain a divisive *created reality* that certain groups are continuous victims. Of course, an individual must suspend logic to believe that members of their group do not engage in the same bad acts as other large groups of individuals. It is an absurdity, because all humanity is imperfect.

This is where the *Dark Empire* and *rogue elements* collide hard against each other. Because of their willingness to expose what is censored, *rogue elements* face a barrage of criticism through the application of various negative *labels* directed against them. These emotionally embedded *labels* are ones that have been planted within the minds of the masses over the course of time. Such labels make it clear how to view *rogue elements* that go about exposing information that does not fit the *created reality* of the continuous victimization of groups.

Altering Reality

The more blatant efforts to divide appear to be well-typified by a particular incident involving NBC, one of the *central controllers* of *viewing screens,* which through happenstance came to light for all to see. This television network altered the content of an emergency phone call relating to the tragic killing of a youth of one race by a Neighborhood Watch person of another race. In this case the altering of the emergency call made it appear that the Neighborhood Watch person was targeting the young man because he was of a certain race. However, the unaltered version of the tape made such a conclusion impossible to reach. Here's how the edited version went.

(Neighborhood Watch person [Zimmerman]) "This guy looks like he's up to no good. He looks black."

But this is actually what was recorded on the 911 tape before the network altered it.

MANIPULATING MAN

(Neighborhood Watch person [Zimmerman]) "This guy looks like he's up to no good, or on drugs or something. It's raining and he's just walking around, looking about."

(911 operator) "Okay. And this guy, is he white, black, or Hispanic?"

(Neighborhood Watch person) "He looks black."[11]

In line with the thesis of *ideological cleansing,* those selected to work within the all-powerful editing room of this network went out of their way to *create a reality* that was highly divisive. Interestingly, no one within the network's ranks appeared to object to this action, which resulted in the highly charged and divisive reality being presented. There are several important points to be gleaned here. The first is the divisive nature of the action taken, one that can reasonably be associated with an attempt to divide the masses. Another is that it shows the extent of the mindset of extremism that guides those in control of the *viewing screens*. As discussed earlier, such extremism is to be expected within a *closed ideological system* such as that of the *viewing screens*, which has cleansed its ranks of counterbalancing ideological beliefs. Another observable point is that it was an effort to prevent the masses from reaching a conclusion that was different from a divisive one.

Also of note was that those hired by the network who opted to engage in altering the information were fired only after the episode came to light by *rogue elements*. Though greatly limited in their reach, they stayed after it until the network, in an effort to appear responsible, fired the three individuals involved. This indicates a tacit approval of their actions within the hierarchy of those in control of the *viewing screens*. It is important to note that those three individuals involved were obviously in agreement to alter the tape, since none approached any *rogue element* to expose the action. Finding three people randomly chosen from society who would willingly collude to do such a thing would be difficult, since they would likely all possess a healthy variance in beliefs, making such collusion highly unlikely. They would also likely possess moral and ethical concerns that would stand in the way. It is only within a *closed ideological system* wherein those selected for employment embrace the same ideology that this type of collusion can happen. In fact, considering the extreme nature of their collectively agreed action, they can reasonably be considered extremist in the cause of dividing the masses.

All of this raises yet another question. How likely is it this was the first time the network engaged in altering information before it was presented to the masses? The likelihood is small since the nature of their deception indicated each individual involved possessed a degree of confidence in the other that only develops over the course of time. The confidence exhibited here was that none feared the other two would expose what was being done. And the faith of each that the others would not expose it was well placed, as none did. Such brazenness develops naturally within a *closed ideological system* where there exists no ideological counterweight. Under the *decentralized* press that America enjoyed until the advent of the *viewing screens*, this ability to deceive the nation on a mass scale did not exist. Any such effort at deception within a *decentralized* and thus free press would be rendered impotent because collusion within it was impossible, as noted by de Tocqueville.

Within a free press environment, it would be big news that a television network altered information and then presented it to the masses as fact. But it didn't become big news. In fact, with the exception of a *rogue element,* it was withheld from the masses by the other *centrally controlled* networks in an act of complicity with their fellow ideologues. Such an action of withholding information from the masses fits well with the entire thesis of *ideological cleansing* and should be expected.

As mentioned earlier, the government and the *Dark Empire* are natural allies against the *force of freedom.* As such, within the above incident there was a sub-event that is revealing as well. A particular radical group issued a bounty on the life of the "Neighborhood Watch" person as a form of retribution. Such an action to incite violence is clearly a criminal act. However, the government refused to pursue charges, even though it knew who issued the incentive to violence.[12] The *Dark Empire,* as would be expected if it was engaged in divisive actions, did its part by not delving into this lapse of law enforcement, lending its support to group favoritism, which naturally accentuates group divisions. Within a *decentralized* free press environment, such censorship would have been rendered impossible. But within a *centrally controlled* media, only *rogue elements,* through their limited media, would discuss it.

Increasing Divisions

Another observable phenomenon is that when the U.S. presidency is attained by an individual who embraces the *ideology of control,* there should be an increase, not a decrease, of divisions within the nation. This is because it is natural for those embracing that ideology to break the masses down into groups, thus making the attainment of control easier. The evidence of this, too, is observable. One excellent example of dividing the masses into easily directional groups took place in the 2012 U.S. presidential election, where one of the contenders, President Barack Obama, was highly favored by the *Dark Empire.* This was due to his breaking new ground in his first term in the promotion of the *new moral order*, as well as the *new economic order.*

Over the course of that election year, a major effort was made on the part of President Obama to deepen divisions on the basis of sex, ethnicity, age, and the *new moral order.* The effort to accentuate differences on the basis of sex came through offers of free contraceptives for women working within a particular religion. This accomplished several divisive goals according to this theory. First, it helped divide the masses along the lines of sex, portraying them as victims because the religious organization was not providing them free contraceptives.[13] Added to that was the notion that any not agreeing to this were "at war" against women. Secondly, it reinforced the *new economic order* where benefits are available with someone else paying for them. Lastly, it attacked religion, one of the *forces of freedom*. And when the votes were finally counted, the greatest "gender gap," or division, in history existed in favor of the president in his reelection effort.[14]

President Obama's next effort involved a campaign to divide the masses along the lines of ethnicity through the issuance of an edict which allowed individuals of a certain ethnicity, who had entered the nation illegally, to be reassured that the government would not enforce the immigration laws.[15] The candidate also promoted the *new moral order* by pressing a new moral belief centered on marriage, pleasing those at the forefront in pressing this new moral code upon the masses.[16] Another effort centered on accentuating a generational divide with a concerted effort to offer the youth of the nation delights from the *new economic order* where others pay the bill.[17] Although such efforts to *divide and conquer* have been an effective method for conquest since the days of Philip II, it is difficult to reconcile within a democracy.

Labeling

As the *Dark Empire* has gone about its business of imposing a *new moral order* upon the masses, it has naturally run into opposition. This is understandable since the morals and social mores being replaced are ones Americans embraced continuously since the 1600s. However, such opposition, if left unchecked, could present a formidable obstacle, slowing the process of re-educating the masses. As such, a system of denaturing those opposed to it is necessary and has been implemented by the use of negative *labeling*. How it is done is quite simple. Those who oppose the implementation of the *new moral order* are given a negative *label* by *creating reality* about them through the *viewing screens*. The process of attaching it involves repeating it again and again, over the course of years, until those susceptible to the influence of the *viewing screens* accept the description and begin using it themselves to describe those opposing some element of the *new moral order*. This accomplishes the goal of suppressing dissent against the imposition of these new morals. It also creates a stigmatized group of individuals: those who oppose the process of pressing the new morals into the minds of the masses. Creating such a group causes another group to naturally appear: those who embrace the *new moral order* out of fear of ostracism.

Those who embrace whatever new moral is being introduced are granted the most positive *labels* because they do the will of the *Dark Empire*. They are characterized as good, advanced, and intelligent. Whereas those refusing to accept it are established in the minds of the masses as not good, along with other negative attributes. However, one description that is never applied to those who refuse to conform is that of independent and free, even though such words are typically applied to those who resist being controlled. This *labeling* process extends beyond the masses and impacts politicians as well. Fearing a negative *label* being attached to themselves, and thus not able to gather votes from those who have accepted the *new moral order*, few statesmen show up to do battle for the *force of freedom*. One *label* typically applied against the few politicians that oppose its imposition is that of extremist. And this, of course, carries with it an irony that is hard to miss.

Censorship

What the masses are not told they cannot know. As such, the *Dark Empire* withholds significant amounts of information which counters its *created reality.* Those individuals well-read from a wide variety of sources understand the truthfulness of this statement. But for those who receive their "news" from the *viewing screens,* this statement will be a mystery. Those who doubt the truthfulness of it should go on a reading binge, utilizing many different sources (major newspapers) from across the world for several months, steering clear of the *viewing screens.* Such access is available via the Internet. Then go back and watch the *viewing screen* "news" while continuing to read. One is sure to be amazed by the volume of information being withheld from the masses. Those who do this will probably never again utilize *viewing screen* "news."

Selective Reporting & Distorting

Such "news" sources also engage in the process of *selective reporting.* That process involves carefully choosing what is to be considered news-worthy, which in many cases advances the *new moral order.* Often this is utilized to complement the belief systems being planted in the minds of the masses using entertainment programming. *Selective reporting* also involves carefully choosing who will be interviewed as an expert, with it trending toward those who agree with the *new moral order* and/or greater government control over the lives of the masses. Additionally, *selective reporting* turns a blind eye to much of the ugly behavior coming from a group *manipulated* by the *Dark Empire,* selectively choosing not to see it and therefore censoring such information from the masses. One interesting example of *selective reporting* took place between two popular movements referred to as the Tea Party and Occupy Wall Street. Both appeared on the scene around 2009. The methods used by the *Dark Empire* to depict the two movements to the masses were informative and revealing.

The Tea Party appeared first, rising up in response to dramatic increases in government spending that caused tremendous budget deficits that threatened the financial health of the nation. Also finding its ire was a series of huge government bailouts of large financial corporations that had mismanaged their affairs. Such bailouts, by their nature, socialize the losses of a few by extending them to the masses for payment, effectively disallowing the free enterprise system from naturally removing weak corporations. Under a free enterprise economic model, the few who made those bad decisions would have been allowed to suffer their own losses or even go under. However, that was not done. This resulted in great anger in those stuck with the tab. Being highly motivated, the movement began succeeding in attracting large crowds of like-minded people who attended town hall meetings and held mass rallies. The movement showed no signs of violence nor behaved in any manner that was negative, which made it difficult for a negative *label* to be applied to it via the *viewing screens*. However, because the Tea Party sought a shift in power back to the *force of freedom*, both the government and the *Dark Empire* were instantly opposed to it.[18]

Under the theory that the *Dark Empire* and government are natural allies, one would have expected them to act in concert against this expression from the *force of freedom*, one that would result in a lessening of the power of the government. In fact, that is exactly what happened. Attempts were made to attach the *label* of extremist to the movement in spite of its track record of good behavior and reasonable demands. The *label* was apparently planted with limited success within the minds of some. Frequently, the individuals attacking the movement were government leaders who supported the *ideology of control* with a litany of them appearing on the *viewing screens* to warn the masses against the movement. There also was an attempt to attach other negative *labels*. But their gatherings were so peaceful that finding selective video clips necessary in order to *create a reality* for the *viewing screens* proved difficult. As a result, the first congressional elections held following its birth were historically successful in favor of their expressed goals.

It is difficult to believe that the Tea Party movement is an extremist one based on what they stand for: requesting that the government live within its means and demanding an end to the socializing of bad decisions by others. Rather, since the Tea Party is dedicated to reducing the power of the government, it is in direct conflict with the *Dark Empire*, making the attempt to negatively *label* it virtually guaranteed from the beginning. Also, since it is a movement dominated by the *force of freedom*, there naturally exists a state of conflict between it and the *Dark Empire*. Therefore, with the *Dark Empire* an unnatural sixth *force of order* that has aligned with the government, its response to any Tea Party type of movement is preordained.

This phenomenon was openly demonstrated during a tragic moment in 2012 after a madman randomly shot moviegoers attending a new Batman series movie, *The Dark Knight Rises*, in Aurora, Colorado. A reporter for one of the *centrally controlled* networks told the masses, as they stared into their *viewing screens*, that the gunman appeared to be a member of the local Tea Party movement.[19] The attempt to *create reality* here centered on planting the idea into the minds of the masses that those who challenge the expansion of government control, such as the Tea Party, are dangerous. Of course, the gunman was not a member of the local Tea Party, and eventually the network was forced to retract the statement under pressure from *rogue elements*. But the quick effort to utilize the stunning attack to demonize the movement further demonstrated the success of *ideological cleansing* within the ranks of the *Dark Empire*. Wherein those "qualified" to speak to the masses are intensely opposed to any Tea Party type of movement, even to the point of inferring that their members might commit mass murder. However, such an action of defaming an opponent is a natural reflex from a political ideologue, unable to apply simple reason before assaulting the character of those opposing their political beliefs. Additionally, the "reporter" was not disciplined for his actions, implying tacit approval of his efforts to discredit the movement and showing unity for his actions within the network.

Although such a false accusation by a network is quite newsworthy, only *rogue elements* discussed it. It should also be noted that the anchorman receiving the report from the "reporter," George Stephanopoulos, had been the press secretary of President Clinton, a Democratic president who approved of the *new moral order*. In a final observation, it should be noted that within a *decentralized* and thus, free media, such individuals as the "reporter" or the anchor would probably never have risen to such prominent positions. That is because within a *decentralized* free press environment, it would be highly unlikely either could have found enough free press outlets to give them such widespread notoriety.

Such an effort to impart a highly negative false charge under the decentralized free press de Tocqueville observed could not happen, because collusion was not possible. And since collusion is impossible within a *decentralized* media, any effort by a media outlet to demonize a political movement would have been irrelevant, reaching too few viewers. But such an action within a *centrally controlled* media confirmed what de Tocqueville had observed as one method a "reporter" could employ to influence the masses. He observed that ...

> only in altering or in denaturing the facts that the journalists can acquire some influence for his opinion.

Since it was indicated that the "reporter" looked at various Tea Party websites for the gunman's name after the shooting, it raises yet another question. Why did this network even think to look at those websites seeking his name? That act in itself is extreme and a demonstration of the deep degree of antipathy within its ranks against a political movement that seeks to reduce government control over the masses. It is important to remember that it is government growth and bailouts that were the targets of the Tea Party movement, not the centralization of media. So why would the *Dark Empire* bother to defame such a movement unless it was aligned with the government? It also demonstrates the degree to which *ideological cleansing* has separated those within the *Dark Empire* from the masses in general. Now ask yourself the following question; How many individuals within the masses would have experienced the thought to look at Tea Party websites seeking the name of the gunman? Probably very few would. The reason is the masses are not the ones driving the effort toward greater government control, but the *Dark Empire*. Since the report was broadcast across the entire nation, the retraction that later came could not undo the harm that had already been done, because some will simply believe the initial report regardless of what other information is released later.

As experts in forming public opinion, there is little doubt those involved within the network who engaged in this action knew this well. Such an unjust phenomenon of false accusations is one so many within the masses have experienced in their lives, knowing that once the false accusation has been made against them, some will continue to embrace it in spite of any retraction. But because of the success of *ideological cleansing*, this method of negatively *labeling* one of the *forces of freedom* will occasionally flow naturally from those working within such an *ideological collective*. However, within that tragedy was dark irony. Just as a member of the *Dark Empire* was attempting to create a terrible reality for the masses centered on the event, another member exposed what may have really been behind the killing spree. A star with MTV who goes by the name Diggity Dave reported that a man with the same name as the mass killer, James Holmes, had phoned him twice, a month prior to the massacre.[20] This from a Los Angeles CBS radio affiliate:

> Dave said Holmes, 24, claimed to have watched the trailer [of the movie] more than 100 times. He was obsessed with the violence depicted in the trailer and dismayed that the film's character didn't use bigger guns, according to Dave.[21]

MANIPULATING MAN

The movie, described as a "very sick and dark twist" of the Batman series, used an extremely violent trailer as part of its promotion to the masses. Apparently, the James Holmes who called the MTV actor could not get enough of that violence, asking such questions as "how many people does Batman kill?" and wanting to know if it was "selective killing...[or] does he make a list of people he wants to kill or a mass body count."[22] Dave was convinced it was the same Holmes who carried out the massacre. And for a nation tearfully searching for answers to the killings, such information could fill in some critical blanks. But the *Dark Empire* would not provide it. Only the false accusation against the Tea Party would make its way across the nation, the *centrally controlled viewing screens* careful to *create* the correct *reality*.

The Occupy movement took to the streets after the Tea Party but in much smaller numbers and with a disruptive tendency almost from the start. But because they espoused greater government control over the economy, they immediately engendered the support of the *Dark Empire*. However, they also espoused strong opposition to the bailouts, which on the surface would appear to be in opposition to greater government control. But ironically, the solution they offered against future bailouts was a socialist vision for America, the very economic theory whose implementation was the bailout. This contradiction, of course, received no *viewing screen* scrutiny. Then clarifying any doubts about what economic theory they embraced, the Occupy movement launched a large multi-city protest on May Day, the communist holiday. Also not garnering much *viewing screen* attention was the distinctly anti-Semitic tone to many of their gatherings. Throughout their rallies there existed a spattering of anti-Semitic messages on posters that appeared invisible to the cameras of the *Dark Empire*. This information would largely be withheld from the masses and only reported by some *rogue elements*.[23]

100

Economic Divisions

The division of the masses into groups also extends into the economic realm through the granting of "entitlements" to those who "allege weakness and inability." This does not include individuals who paid into a program with the reasonable expectation of a future return. Since there is a segment of the masses that would prefer to have others pay their bills, myriad government programs have been created to attract them. Once placed within a program, several things occur. Some become controllable with an interest in a continuation of the benefit and, therefore, support ever-greater government control. As a result, many are able to be directed politically to support those who embrace the *ideology of control.*

In the 2012 presidential election, the candidate supported by the *Dark Empire,* President Obama, presented an advertisement that encapsulated the effort to create an economically dependent group based on gender. The effort took form in an advertisement called, "The Life of Julia," which presented a cartoon character as a positive example of her gender's dependency on government assistance. It listed a litany of programs Julia gained access to from the time she was born and throughout her entire life. It was an effort to entice those still independent to take a bite into the apple of dependency. And not to worry-others would be picking up the tab. The message was an attempt to *create reality* for those within her group to support more government control.[24]

Religion

Because of their lack of life experiences to draw upon for discernment, one of the groups most able to be *manipulated* is the young. Across nature, it is the young who are sought as the easiest prey, partly because of this lack of life experiences. As such, since the time of the first colonists until the 1950s, there existed a kind of covering over many of them, providing a form of protection while they gained the life experiences that would provide them the discernment necessary for self-defense. That protection came in the form of deeply held *rigid religious beliefs* handed down from their parents, the same morals and social mores de Tocqueville had observed. And it is such *rigid religious beliefs* where despotism finds its match. Therefore, to carve out the youth of the nation as a group capable of being *manipulated*, it was necessary to replace those *rigid religious beliefs* with something more malleable. As a result, of the four *forces of freedom,* it is religion that appears to have caught the special attention of the *Dark Empire.* de Tocqueville had rightly observed the powerful impact religion had in sustaining freedom and democracy in America, noting its immediate impression on him.

> It was the religious aspect of the country that first struck my eye.

He noted how different it was than what existed in Europe, and that,

> In America one sees one of the <u>freest</u> and most enlightened peoples in the world eagerly fulfill all the external duties of religion. (Emphasis added)

Then he observed the intimate connection between religion in America, and freedom.

> Among us, I had seen the spirit of religion and the spirit of freedom almost always move in contrary directions. Here I found them <u>united intimately with one another: they reigned together on the same soil</u>. (Emphasis added)

Of course, it is religion that provided America its mores and morals that de Tocqueville found absolutely essential in maintaining democracy in America.

... I consider mores to be one of the greatest general causes to which the maintenance of a democratic republic in the United States can be attributed.

Then he expounds further on this concept of mores.

... not only do I apply it to mores properly so-called, which one could call habits of the heart, but to the different notions that men possess, to various opinions that are current in their midst, and to the sum of ideas of which the habits of the *mind* are formed. (Emphasis added)

Years before de Tocqueville wrote those words, various Founding Fathers had expressed similar thoughts as to the importance of religion for the sustaining of democracy. John Adams, the second president and a signer of the Declaration of Independence, stated,

Our Constitution was made only for a moral people and a religious people. It is wholly inadequate to the government of any other.[25]

Adding to that he states,

It is religion and morality alone which can establish the principles upon which freedom can securely stand. The only foundation of a free constitution is pure virtue.[26]

From Benjamin Rush, a signer of the Declaration of Independence,

The only foundation for ... a republic is to be laid in Religion. Without this there can be no virtue, and without virtue there can be no liberty ...[27]

and John Witherspoon of the Continental Congress,

He is the best friend to American liberty, who is most sincere and active in promoting true and undefiled religion ...[28]

MANIPULATING MAN

These few statements are but a tiny sample of a virtual avalanche of similar words from an array of Founding Fathers, all leading to the same inevitable conclusion: that whether American democracy endures will be determined by whether the religious and social mores of the masses can be sustained. It is these same morals and social mores that de Tocqueville observed years later, writing about them in his classic work, *Democracy in America*. In fact, it is this same moral foundation that the *Dark Empire* has been methodically replacing with its *new moral order*, and for good reason. Because those religious beliefs were so rigid, they allowed no space for *manipulation*. Without the malleable beliefs of the *new moral order*, which creates the ability to *manipulate* the masses, despotism is hopefully outmatched. The Founding Fathers saw this clearly.

Because rigid morals and religious beliefs create an impenetrable barrier against tyranny, it has sustained the greatest assault from the *Dark Empire* of all the *forces of order*. A natural consequence of the *Dark Empire's* constant denaturing of religion is that it has assisted in the breakup of another *force of order*, the family, which also assists in isolating the young.

The religion de Tocqueville and the Founding Fathers were referring to, of course, is that of Judo/Christianity, which has dominated North America since the first settlers arrived. It is foundational within both faiths that there is an objective truth relating to morality. In other words, that which is deemed as good or bad is already largely decided for those who practice these faiths. They simply choose to accept it or reject it, but the subjective option of altering it does not exist. Such rigid beliefs are the *Dark Empire's* worst nightmare, making *manipulation* and control extremely difficult, and in some cases impossible to achieve. This is because they must negotiate past unalterable standards. That is why it has been so important to undermine such inflexible moral beliefs and replace them with a set of morals that are subjective and primarily based on feelings. It also explains why a kind of designer religion has evolved for some within the masses, allowing them greater moral flexibility in an effort to juggle the *new moral order* within a traditional religious structure. Therefore, the *Dark Empire* has employed the *viewing screens* to portray those who continue to embrace rigid morality and religion as being weak-minded, inferring that they are too simplistic to determine truth for themselves. This is unlike those they promote as the more advanced thinkers-individuals whose moral bearings have great flexibility. With "superpowers" over the minds of the youth, it is they who have felt the greatest impact from the drive to replace the objective sense of morality with a more flexible one based on feelings, leaving them the most vulnerable to *manipulation*. Such a flexible moral belief system is the foundation of the *new moral order*.

In a study conducted in 2008 by the eminent Notre Dame sociologist Christian Smith, the team he led conducted interviews with 230 young adults across America. The study was dedicated to mapping the guidance systems young people employed in determining morality. The interviewees began by asking open-ended questions relating to the meaning of life, what is right and wrong, as well as various moral dilemmas in order to draw from them the depth of their thoughts on questions deeply pondered by Americans since the earliest days. David Brooks, writing for *The New York Times* about the study, would point out Smith's conclusion that such questions produced rambling answers with the young people, "groping for anything sensible [to say] on these matters." Smith continued by saying that "not many of them have previously given much or any thought to many of the kinds of questions about morality that we asked."[29]

The following answers typify the thinking of the group and represent individuals whose moral compass is set to nothing but their feelings. Morality was a matter of taste or as many would respond, "It's up to the individual. Who am I to say?" The study would also record such deep moral ponderings as, "I would do what I thought made me happy or how I felt. I have no other way of knowing what to do but how I internally feel." Another typical respondent put it this way. "I mean, I guess what makes something right is how I feel about it. But different people feel different ways, so I couldn't speak on behalf of anyone else as to what's right and wrong."[30] Essentially, these youths, who possess technology that enables them to access any part of the globe instantaneously, would be incapable of holding their own in a moral philosophical debate with their counterparts from the 1600s, 1700s, 1800s, and for the most part, the 1900s.

After the scathing article came out, *The New York Times* published a response from a young woman named Valarie, the director of a "social action initiative," allowing her to rebut the observations Brooks' made based on the study. Unwittingly confirming Brooks' main thesis that her generation lacks an objective sense of morality, she pointed out that her generation won't "frame our moral commitments in the black-and-white language of previous generations, because we've inherited the damage that comes from absolutes." Ignoring the easy observation of society dis- integrating all around her as it, coincidentally, moves away from those absolutes, she proudly went on to proclaim why her generation has none. She then goes on to observe the other benefit of possessing no absolute moral vision, unwittingly confirming why the *Dark Empire* has found it necessary to denature the masses of any form of objective sense of moral- ity that comes from the Judo/Christian faith. In her conclusion she states her generation would,

> ... rather channel our diverse moral stirrings into meaningful action.[31]

Since there is no absolute morality within the *new moral order* they embrace, then the only way she and others like her can experience any moral meaning to their lives is through *"meaningful action."* In other words, many within her generation are completely able to be directed toward some actionable goal as a replacement for the application of any form of objective morality. They are, therefore, the opposite of those with rigid moral bearings who are virtually unable to be *manipulated*. But these individuals that follow the *new moral order* (no absolutes) and if properly convinced, are able to be pointed toward *meaningful action* through *created reality*. And this phenomenon is not, by any means, limited to the youth. It is only that they provide the best example of those easiest *manipulated*, since most lack a depth of past experiences to draw upon for discernment. It is only through a compass guided by the objective morality of the Judo/Christian faiths that *created reality* meets its match, unable to direct those staring into their *viewing screens* to be herded into *meaningful action*.

By using the *viewing screens* to press the *new moral order* into the minds of the masses, the *Dark Empire* has prepared them for *manipulation*, able to be directed toward any *meaningful action* that has associated with it a good feeling. This is possible because the individual so afflicted no longer has a sturdy moral reference point from which to form independent judgments that supersede feelings. By *creating a reality* for those neutered of the rigid morals of their ancestors, these individuals are easily led into embracing any cause, as long as it is well packaged to *create a reality* that it is a worthy one. But because the *Dark Empire* controls so much of the content coming across the *viewing screens*, such individuals are susceptible to *manipulation*. Their condition is similar to that of a buoy used for guidance in a storm, as opposed to a lighthouse. It is a lighthouse that retains a rigid fixed position, providing a sturdy reference, guiding ships safely around the lurking dangers of a coast such as reefs and shoals. But a buoy, not rigidly placed, is capable of being cast about by any powerful current or wind, causing those who would attempt to use it as a reference point to be carried into dangerous waters.

MANIPULATING MAN

Therefore, it is the non-subjective morality found within the Judo/ Christian faiths that had to be destroyed if the *Dark Empire* were to make headway in establishing its control over the minds of the youth, as well as many within the masses as a whole. This explains why religion has come under unrelenting assault through the *viewing screens*. It also explains why the *new moral order* was necessary, because something had to replace the stubborn morals of religion so the door to *manipulation* could be opened. And how successful has the process of replacing those religious beliefs with the *new moral order* been? An event during the 2012 Democratic National Convention, gathering to nominate President Obama for a second term, would appear to reveal that answer.

National political conventions tend to bring together a concentration of the ruling hierarchy of a political party in one place at one time, thus representing a grand gathering of those in charge. Since political conventions take place only once every four years, competition to become a delegate is usually fierce, with only those possessing real political clout able to make their way in. As such, it is a concentrated representation of those in charge of the party, essentially a gathering of its true believers. But occasionally an unscripted moment will present itself, allowing the true nature of those gathered to be revealed. And so it was at the 2012 convention.

During the course of national political conventions, a "platform" is established representing the position of the party on a host of issues of importance to voters. Once voted on and passed by the delegates, it becomes party policy. However, in 2012 it would be noteworthy by what was omitted from it more so than by what was included. For the first time in the history of the Democratic Party there was no reference to "God" within their platform.

The president's opponents pounced upon the omission, forcing the gathering Democrats to declare it to be nothing more than an honest mistake. But a problem existed in using that as an excuse. As efforts to create a party platform at conventions take place, inevitably the previous platform established only four years earlier is always taken into consideration. However, that platform had included references to "God." Therefore, the omission in the 2012 platform could only be the result of an act of removal. Caught in a tight political spot, the party offered an amendment to add the reference back in. But no longer could it be done privately in a secluded conference room. It would now have to go before the convention floor and receive a voice vote from the thronging delegates. According to the Internet news site Huffington Post, this is what happened next.

> But when Los Angeles Mayor Antonio Villaraigosa, the convention chairman, came to the podium to ask for the approval of the delegates, those who shouted opposition to the language change were as loud, if not louder, than those who voiced their support.
>
> Villarigosa, in what quickly became an awkward moment, asked for the voice vote three more times in all. After the second time, he paused for several seconds and looked behind him for guidance from a convention staffer—possibly a parliamentarian—before turning back and asking for a third vote.
>
> Even though the nos were again as loud if not louder than the ayes on the third vote, Villaraigosa said he had determined that two-thirds of those present had voted in favor. [In response] boos filled the arena.[32]

This event raises a simple question. Why would the most powerful members of a political party gathered at their convention seek to erase any reference of God from their platform? The answer can be given in one word: control. Within a party which has become the focal point of an increasingly aggressive drive to promote the *new moral order* and the *new economic order*, any reference that counters the notion of flexible morals results in a natural response against it. Accordingly, the booing was sincere.

Stars

Yet another controllable group springs forth from the *Dark Empire*. By controlling who becomes famous via the *viewing screens*, there exists a large group of individuals who the masses know and trust who embrace the *new moral order*. Since the masses look up to these stars and seek to be like them, when they speak, it carries great influence. These stars are the ones who fill the roles played in popular entertainment programming, which is often designed to re-educate the masses toward acceptance of moral beliefs rejected by their ancestors for centuries. By continuously playing programming that presents an aspect of the *new moral order* as good, it becomes reality for the masses and creates a shift in beliefs. This takes place even if the morals being reversed are ones that had been embraced by their ancestors since the earliest days, because there is simply no ability of some to resist the power of repetitious suggestion coming from those they see on the *viewing screens*.

❈   ❈   ❈   ❈   ❈

As the masses stare into their *viewing screens,* their minds are absorbed into *created reality*, unable to prevent the absurd from entering their essence. No longer possessing the freedom of mind that distinguished their ancestors, many have lost the capacity of free will so critical to operating a democracy. Unlike the despotic forces in the olden days that satisfied their cravings by controlling the productiveness of the masses, it is now their minds that are demanded. It is their minds technology has given them, ushering in a new *age of manipulation*. It is the advent of technology that has finally enabled the despotic forces that have always lurked within the shadows of obscurity to join their efforts, finally able to establish that which their ideological ancestors had always sought: a form of aristocracy over the masses of North America. The result is that America is no longer a democracy, having been rendered to only an idea of what it once was.

Out of the smoke and dust of it all has risen up a new man whose bond to his ancestors is diminished. He has been taught to embrace a *new moral order* that was anathema to those who came before him. He appears incapable of connecting its implementation to the decay he sees all around. His mind is carefully guided to ignore results and to suspend simple logic. He is easily *manipulated* through emotionally charged *labels*. To him, the *rogue element* is dangerous and should be shut down or limited in its reach. He is the new man, one that in a real sense does not know himself or whom he was destined to become. Many of his opinions are voiced almost word-for-word to what he has been told is the correct way to think. Debating him is usually fruitless as emotionally embedded *labels* have been so deeply planted within his mind that it has become almost impenetrable. He is, sadly, able to be directed by those with the power to craft the correct messages across the *viewing screens,* causing him a fatal certainty in the reality that has been created for him.

CHAPTER EIGHT

The Rise of the Drones

It was on Sunday evening October 30, 1938, when the first big success in *manipulating* the masses took place in America. Radio had taken the nation by storm, becoming the first mass communications medium in history, providing free entertainment and news for those who bought one of the new devices. And buy they did, with most homes possessing one by the end of that year. However, that evening the new *centrally controlled* medium would flex a muscle of influence over the minds of the masses which few realized it possessed. Listeners who tuned in to the Columbia Broadcasting System discovered, much to their delight, that music from Ramon Raquello and his orchestra was being piped in live from New York City. At least that's what they had been told to believe.

As the beat of the band streaked across the firmament from sea to shining sea, those listening could imagine animated couples dancing at the Hotel Park Plaza, where the orchestra was said to be located. Out across the nation and down lonely country roads, farm girls listening to the show could imagine being swept off their feet on a dance floor in a city they could see only in their dreams. But Prince Charming and the serenity of the music would be rudely interrupted that evening in America by none other than the planet Mars.

A special bulletin stopped the orchestra dead in its tracks, reporting that the Mount Jennings Observatory in Chicago had spotted explosions on the surface of the Martian planet. It was a brief interruption, with the listeners quickly returning to the melodious sounds of Ramon Raquello. But it was an omen of things to come that evening. Ultimately what would unfold over the course of the next hour would drive an estimated one million people onto the highways and byways, especially in New York and New Jersey, to escape the impending doom they were assured was coming. It seems that Martians had invaded the East Coast of the United States and were beginning to move westward, bringing their destruction with them. As people fled, many loaded up their cars, believing their departure could be a long one. The more thoughtful brought wet towels as protection against the "poison gas" they were told was being used by the unwelcomed visitors. In Newark, doctors and nurses began volunteering their services to help those still alive in the affected areas. On the other side of the continent, in San Francisco, an excited resident would exclaim, "My God, where can I volunteer my service? We've got to stop this thing!"[1]

After the night of terror was over, the front page headline of *The New York Times* would sum up what had really happened:

> Radio Listeners in Panic, Taking War Drama As Fact. Many Flee Homes to Escape 'Gas Raid from Mars' – Phone Calls Swamp Police at Broadcast of Wells Fantasy.[2]

Ironically, the entire show was nothing more than a radio version of H.G. Wells' popular book, *War of the Worlds* being presented by the

Mercury Theatre to its radio listeners across the nation. At the beginning of the show, Orson Welles, the brain of the project, had announced that the listener was about to hear a theatrical rendition of the book. But for those who happened to miss that bit of information, what followed would reveal the awesome power of *centrally controlled* mass communications, able to direct the minds of the masses, rendering them under the spell of those in charge.

It takes a lot to drive people from their homes and into the streets on a sleepy Sunday evening. But on that chilly day in late October 1938, the *creation of reality* was so powerful that those under its influence became totally controlled by those creating it. And all of it was accomplished through the use of radio, a mass medium capable of sending nothing more than sound into the homes of the masses.

In the case of the *War of the Worlds* broadcast, those who were duped would soon discover the truth that no invasion had occurred, allowing them to recover their sense of stability, with dignity coming much later. And probably knowing they had been fooled, some would develop a healthy skepticism of what they were told to believe in the future. Interestingly, any listeners who had applied simple logic and observational skills to the event could have noted how fanciful the whole thing was, since individuals within the unfolding drama were arriving at distant locations within only a matter of minutes. They had to because the show was only an hour long! But for many, once emotion takes over, logic begins to recede.

Less than a year later, just before the start of World War II, it would become the German people's turn to suffer mass *manipulation*. The Nazis, skilled in *creating a reality* for the German masses, instituted "Operation Canned Goods," a false flag operation designed to create the appearance that Poland had attacked Germany, thus providing a pretext for the German invasion of that peaceful country.[3] And within Germany the masses overwhelmingly believed what they were being told. However, any who applied simple logic would have questioned it. Why would so inferior a military power as Poland, with about 1,000,000 men under arms, attack the German Wehrmacht, the most powerful military in Europe, with 20,000,000 in its ranks?[4] Obviously, the question resolves itself. But with a high degree of emotion woven into the *created reality*, the Nazi puppet masters were able to *manipulate* the German masses toward any conclusion they wanted.

With the spreading of *viewing screens* across America, the perfect vehicle for *manipulating* the masses suddenly appeared within every home in the land. As those embracing the *ideology of control* came to dominate the ranks of the new *centrally controlled* mass medium, *manipulation* of the masses that once was only a historical curiosity soon became the norm. Having succeeded over the course of several decades in bringing large elements of the masses to follow their *new moral order*, the nation became further divided into sub-groups based on degrees of acceptance. But for those who stubbornly continue to hold on to the old system of moral beliefs, in spite of the unrelenting attacks against them through the *viewing screens,* they are treated to sustained assaults against their character. Yet what they embrace created the foundation of the most successful society in world history in terms of stability, freedom, and prosperity.

While some continue to resist the implementation of the *new moral order*, others have succumbed to the unrelenting drum beat driven into their minds through the *viewing screens*. However, unlike those who were fooled by the Wells drama, the *manipulation* they experience spans the course of years, not just a single hour. As such, they have, in a sense, been *absorbed* into *created reality,* programmed to parrot back acceptance often word-for-word of what the *viewing screens* have told them to believe. Another effect of this *absorption* is that simplistic logic appears to have been suspended through a technique of attaching high emotion to the new morals being pressed. The end result has been to replace a normal logic-based system of discernment that includes some emotion with one where emotion overwhelms logic, making them vastly easier to *manipulate*.

As a result, within the masses has arisen a new group, one that did not exist before the time of the *viewing screens*. Having been brought to a created mindset through the repetitiveness of *created reality*, they are now as easy to control as those who fled Martians. Adding to their plight is the personal possession of high technology, granting them the self-delusion of both freedom and knowledge. But because they lack discernment, their devices are turned against their own minds, reinforcing the *created reality* that now controls them. For the lack of a better term to describe them, they have become living *Drones* at the disposal of the *Dark Empire*, capable of being directed toward virtually any form of thinking their masters determine is needed. Along with others who have suffered this fate, together they have risen up as a new force, a legion of *Drones* directed by and at the disposal of the *Dark Empire*. However, even though their numbers are significant, they do not represent a *force of order* within their own right because they appear to have limited independent direction. But they strengthen the *Dark Empire* in its efforts to overcome the *forces of freedom* within America.

Drone Observations

Because they embrace the *new moral order*, *Drones* are made to see themselves as the vanguard of a new and advanced way of thinking. They see themselves as the wave of the future because they have seen the steady implementation of the *new moral order* over the course of time. But employing such an observation to confirm the rightness of a belief system is deceptive, since progressive degeneration also leaves an observable trail over time. The real test of its worthiness is the progressive impact its implementation has had on society. And that is where the *Drone* must suspend logic. By applying simplistic logic to the results derived from the implementation of the *new moral order,* an insurmountable obstacle to faith in it is presented. Since the advent of *centrally controlled viewing screens,* and the promotion of this *new moral order* through them, the decay of society witnessed through a multitude of social ills, almost completely unknown to their ancestors, is clearly observable. But those under the spell of *manipulation* are hard pressed to connect a logical sequence, especially when strong emotion has been woven within the message.

In embracing the *new economic order,* which entails greater government control bringing the nation in the direction of socialism, it is much the same story. A simple comparison of the results experienced by a free enterprise system, one without socialistic bailouts of large corporations that made bad decisions, versus the more socialistic economic model, leaves no doubt as to which has improved the lot of the masses more. Yet the *Drone* continues to believe in greater government control, often repeating the mantra that the European socialistic model is the way to go.

For decades those who promote the *new economic order* have assured *Drones* that a European-style social democracy would be preferable to that which has existed in America since its earliest days. Such enlightenment from Europe was to usher in an age of social delights delivered from the government to the waiting arms of the masses, advancing society toward some form of utopia. But there was always a problem with the whole idea. Someone had to pay for it. Certainly those receiving the benefits of the labor of others and were able-bodied would now produce less, which is exactly what a host of West European nations experienced.

Finally, in 2011, 2012, and 2013, like huge dominos, the financial systems of a multitude of nations across Europe began to crack under the strain of this *new economic order.* Unfolding before an amazed and fearful world, one after another approached default on their debts in rapid succession. Eventually, in an act of desperation, those Europeans in charge of the mess floated the idea of confiscating between 6.75% and 9.99% of the savings of individuals held within banks located in the small nation of Cyprus. Apparently, their understanding of economics did not inform them that mentioning such an idea for one country would immediately lead savers elsewhere to question the safety of their funds, thus, making the problem potentially even worse.[5] However, although this represented the inevitable end result of the *new economic order* being implemented within a modern economy, it did not represent a "teachable" moment for most *Drones.*

Part of the effort to establish the *new economic order* is by establishing the notion that those who built successful businesses are not truly responsible for that success, but that society as a whole somehow participated. The logic goes something like this. Since the business had to use roads built by society in order to function, it owes some debt to it greater than the taxes it pays. Of course, this ignores the fact that business provides the jobs that produce the taxes that built the roads in the first place. It also ignores the fact that the government risked nothing to establish the business, nor did it reimburse those who risked much to establish a business and lost it all. But the whole concept that entrepreneurs did not build their businesses does not appear to be a true debate in the sense that honest differences exist between two opposing sides. Rather, it appears to be an attempt to *create reality* in the minds of those susceptible to it. It is about pure control by those who embrace the *ideology of control* in their effort to undermine free enterprise, because such freedom creates individuals independent from, and almost always opposed to, the *ideology of control.*

The thinking associated with the notion that business owners are not really responsible for their business success represents a critical leap for the implementation of the *new economic order.* This is because it seeks to establish that all privately owned businesses should socialize their profits, which then provides more funds at the disposal of the government for distribution. This, of course, empowers the government further. But a moral rationale for taking it must be provided. Simply taking it on the basis they want it will not do. By *creating reality* for the masses that those with successful businesses are not morally due the profits, but society as a whole is, a moral rationale is provided to those capable of accepting it. This effort was seen in the 2012 presidential election when the candidate strongly supported by the *Dark Empire,* President Barack Obama, told business owners they "didn't build" their businesses alone, but that society was partly responsible.[6]

Other traits associated with these *Drones* are worth noting, with most possessing many of them. Because the *Dark Empire* has driven its ideology into their minds using high emotion, most *Drones* place greater importance on their ideology instead of freedom. When there is a conflict between freedom and ideology, they will invariably choose ideology. This is why they see no wrong in those who embrace their ideology, taking over what was once a free press. Further, they are hard-pressed to find fault in the promotion of the *new moral order* by their fellow believers, utilizing the media they took over. On the other hand, any effort by the *forces of freedom* to fend off the *new moral order* is typically viewed by *Drones* as a real danger to society. This is seen in the battle over free speech. *Drones* tend to give blanket approval to all pornographic expressions, but recoil against any political free speech that crosses the *new moral order.*

Since *rogue elements* represent a real and present danger to the *Dark Empire's* effort to *create reality,* it has resulted in highly negative *labels* attached to them, and then emotionally pressed into the mind of the *Drone.* Because of this, it is highly unlikely that a *Drone* will gather information from a *rogue element* with the intent of gaining insight from it. Most appear to believe *rogue elements* are not good sources for information and are even dangerous because they discuss observations or information the *Dark Empire* has assured them are not true, or do not exist. Since in many cases the *Drone* has been told that certain things do not exist, then these *rogue elements* must not be telling the truth. All observations or information that *Drones* are told does not exist will always undermine some aspect of the *created reality* of *new moral order* or the *new economic order*. Also, when the opportunity presents itself, any significantly damaging information relating to highly placed political leaders who embrace the *ideology of control* will be deemed as not newsworthy.

The power of the *label* over the mind of a *Drone* is immense. Such *labeling* is utilized to fine-tune their beliefs, capable of directing them toward *meaningful action* for or against a group, individual, or issue of the day. Each *label* has associated with it an emotional charge planted over the course of time deep within their mind. A true *Drone* cannot resist a *label*. Once a *label* is employed, some will begin issuing certain phrases they have been assured make them intelligent. Some of these phrases on the surface sound intelligent, but when they are delved into, they fall apart. Challenging a *Drone* on a *label* is an act of futility directly related to the depth of emotion used to implant it within their mind.

Many believe themselves to be highly intelligent because of what they believe, not because of the results those beliefs bring. They appear to be inoculated against receiving information that counters what they have been told to believe. It is noteworthy that only a few *Drones* can articulate the details of what they want done and why. The vast majority are relegated to the use of emotionally charged political statements in response to detailed challenges. Because they employ emotion instead of logic as their primary method for discernment, they will, on occasion, unwittingly provide information that refutes their own stated beliefs. This is possible because certain statements they express represent a highly emotional concept to them, which causes the contradicting logic behind it to be hidden from their mind.

With the *ideology of control* dividing the masses into groups, many *Drones* have been placed within some favored group or have been taught to support one. Groups are very important to these *Drones*, because the *Dark Empire* has emotionally pressed into their minds, often in the form of guilt, that they must be favored. This is, of course, a highly divisive act since it differentiates individuals within that group from society as a whole. All *Drones* within a group are emotionally charged to support members of their group first, subtly relegating the interests of the nation as secondary. Because many *Drones* have been isolated into one of the "favored" groups, most appear to be easily herded toward any *meaningful action* the *Dark Empire* embraces. *Drones* within a group are the easiest to *manipulate*.

This all plays out when a member of a group that embraces the *new moral order* and the *new economic order* seeks public office. Everyone who votes for them is not a *Drone*. But almost all *Drones* will vote for them. The key is they support the *new order,* otherwise they represent a *rogue element,* and will be subtly marked for attack by the *Dark Empire,* causing most *Drones* to be opposed to them. All politicians falling in line with the *new order* will receive the blessings of the *Dark Empire,* which will result in two advantages being bestowed upon them. First, legions of *Drones* will be directed to vote for them, and, secondly, a very limited "vetting" effort will be done on their background. This vetting involves the natural free press tendency to delve into key life events, like past experiences and associations of the politician in order to bring an understanding to the voters of who the candidate really is. There is an inverse relationship between the extent of vetting done by the *Dark Empire* and the level of political office being sought by a politician who supports the *ideology of control*. That is to say that the higher the office sought, the less looking into their background will take place.

Neither high IQ nor advanced education appears to prevent the creation of a *Drone*. In the case of higher education, in some instances, it assists in the making of one. This phenomenon is a result of the degree of success the *ideology of control* has experienced in moving certain universities from being centers of free thought to bastions of the *new moral order* through the process of *ideological cleansing*. As such, college graduates from certain universities now appear to simply parrot both the *new moral order* as well as the *new economic order* with little consideration of the results both have produced. In a unique paradox, perhaps for the first time in history, a number of individuals with higher education are surpassed, in a general understanding of how things really work, by a number of individuals without it. And this strange paradox is something new under the sun. This odd phenomenon is purely a result of the power of the *viewing screens* in league with *ideological cleansing* that has taken place within certain universities. It is also a reflection of the fact that *rogue elements* still exist as sources for information. Otherwise this juxtaposition, which may have never previously existed, would be impossible to take place. The simple conclusion from this is that the salient factor determining if a person is able to be made into a *Drone* comes down to their ability to resist *absorption*, not education or IQ.

For the *Dark Empire*, certain "educational" institutions have become breeding grounds for the creation of *Drones*. They are universities where a fervent believer in the *ideology of control* reached the top position. Such individuals, once highly placed, begin the process of purging the faculty of those who espouse any set of beliefs other then the *new moral order* as well as the *new economic order*. No other explanation does justice to the myriad studies reflecting their increasing ideological purity. Such brazen actions representing the process of *ideological cleansing* are enacted over the course of time and are to be a natural expectation of those who embrace the *ideology of control*. These universities are identifiable by their lack of traditional-thinking professors. As a result, the *Drones* (students) produced by these facilities are ready to begin *meaningful action* unfettered by results.

Considering the litany of economic carnage resulting from the implementation of the *new economic order* and the societal disintegration from pressing the *new moral order* upon the masses, it is necessary to alter the frame of reference from which a *Drone* views what is good. Essentially, they must be driven away from utilizing results in validating the beliefs pressed into their mind. Therefore, in order to eliminate the natural tendency of considering results in the determination of the worthiness of any *meaningful action*, *Drones* are made to process information by feelings. The process of accomplishing this involves *viewing screens* continuously pressing emotionally charged concepts into their minds over the course of time, until their reaction to information bypasses results. With the exception of those who embrace *designer religion*, individuals who possess strong traditional religious beliefs are vastly less likely to fall prey to this since they embrace a set of non-subjective notions of right and wrong. This makes them much more difficult to *manipulate* toward *meaningful action* than those who utilize feelings to confirm beliefs. Thus, the creation of *Drones* is another reason why the *Dark Empire* has utilized so much *viewing screen* time toward purging traditional religious beliefs out of the masses. By replacing them with a subjective set of emotionally driven morality, encompassed within the *new moral order, Drone* creation becomes possible.

Since they are more apt to employ their feelings in determining what is good, *Drones* are provided some simplistic concepts to help them fend off attacks on the *created reality* that the *new moral order* is superior to the traditional religious beliefs it has replaced. Since the *created reality* that the *new moral order* has benefited society more than traditional beliefs runs so hard against easily observable results, a mixture of information combined with emotion is used to inoculate the *Drone* against this threat. A typical example of this technique is the *Drone* being taught about some historical wrong that was perpetrated in the name of religion and is reassured that the *new moral order* would never allow such a thing to happen, thus, proving its moral superiority. But here is where the *Drone's* lack of logic plus information gets the better of him. Since all institutions, including religious ones, possess moments in their past they wish could be forgotten, all can be criticized. But, of course, that misses the bigger picture, which is exactly why the *Drone* is provided limited, emotionally laced information, rendering him unable to see the forest for its trees. In the above case, it is like criticizing one who might have misguidedly set a house on fire, while ignoring those who have set an entire city ablaze for the purpose of control. And the implementation of the *new moral order* has, indeed, set the entire nation ablaze with rampant crime and an assortment of social ills that under the social mores it replaced were almost non-existent. But to the *Drone,* such logic is elusive.

Drones see *institutional absorption* as a right and appear to target religion-related institutions with a special zeal. Any resistance against their efforts to absorb an institution results in a deluge of *labeling* from the *Drone* against those resisting. Typically, the *Dark Empire* will present an act of *institutional absorption* as a great crusade, giving the *Drone* a purpose. Thus, once placed within the mind of the *Drone* that the effort to *absorb* the institution is a crusade, directing them toward *meaningful action* is easy.

Most *Drones* believe that opposing the *new moral order* is not a moral act, even though such opposition was the norm for centuries. As such, they have mentally cut ties with their ancestors on a host of beliefs, which is necessary in order to justify the imposition of moral concepts that were anathema to those who came before them.

Since the "news" derived from the *viewing screens* lacks effective criticism of the *new order,* the *Drone* is protected from challenges against their world view. Although this is true, it is important to understand that many *Drones* believe they are highly informed. An excellent example of this phenomenon was seen during the "Arab Spring" that occurred in early 2011. As the Arab masses, particularly in Egypt, threw off the yoke of long-time dictators, the *Dark Empire created reality* that it was a grand democratic expression that would transform that nation into a true democracy. In contrast, *rogue elements* presented the perspective that it was much more likely that the Egyptian dictator would be replaced with something much worse, a radical Islamic regime. Then when the dust finally settled, the fallen dictator was replaced with something much worse, a radical Islamic regime.[6] In spite of this example being replicated within countless events, *Drones* appear incapable of discerning that the source from which they receive information is lacking. The reason for this appears to be that the emotionally embedded concept that *rogue elements* are bad is more powerful than their natural desire for accurate information. It also indicates that the *Drone* has accumulated an emotional investment in sustaining the *created reality* that *rogue elements* are bad and that they, the *Drones,* are the ones who truly know what is going on.

There is more to be gleaned from the so-called "Arab Spring" event. Since both President Obama and his Secretary of State, Hillary Clinton, threw their support behind it, the *Dark Empire created reality* that it was a grand democratic expression by the masses in the Middle East. This was done in order to protect those two highly placed political leaders who embrace the *ideology of control.* As the dust from that tumultuous event began to settle, the ultimate impact of their support resulted in an American ally, Egypt, being taken over by the Muslim Brotherhood, an avowed American enemy. Since Egypt is the most populous Arab state in the troubled region, such a reversal of fortunes represented a significant foreign policy disaster resting on the doorstep of both politicians. However, because both embrace the *ideology of control,* the *Dark Empire* did not allow either to suffer the consequences of their actions in line with the degree that political disaster represented. Both appeared securely protected from being effectively linked to their own failure, even though it was one of historical proportions. This type of protection is provided only to those who embrace the *ideology of control,* allowing a *created reality* of competency to be sustained. When *rogue elements* point out such events, *Drones* are assured their criticisms are not true.

        ✿   ✿   ✿   ✿   ✿

Because *Drones* embrace the moral flexibility of the *new moral order,* this makes it easier for them to be *manipulated.* But that is not the only phenomenon associated with this embrace. Since their morality is relative to feelings instead of being based on rigid concepts, the ability to engage in acts that were previously determined to be immoral allows them to embrace concepts such as, "the ends justify the means," far easier than those embracing the old rigid morals. As such, they see no immorality utilizing the *viewing screens* to promote a *new moral order* over the masses. Such flexible moral beliefs also allow for the withholding of significant information from the masses, replacing an inherent professional trust with that of ideology. Within those who hold to traditional rigid morals, such an action would be difficult to justify.

Since *Drones* are individuals who have been *absorbed* into the *created reality* of the *Dark Empire,* and sadly able to be *manipulated* toward *meaningful action,* it raises the question of how this takes place. Dr. Philip Zimbardo, who was quoted in a previous chapter for his famous "Stanford Prison Experiment," and has received more than 24 awards, served on 20 boards, authored more than 20 psychology textbooks, and written over 120 journal articles, would appear to answer that question.[8] In researching religious cults, he would conclude that the core of human choice includes volition, commitment, and responsibility, and that mind control is similar to socialization. Socialization is the key word here.

> When information is systematically hidden, withheld, or distorted, people may end up making biased decisions, even though they believe that they are freely choosing to act.[9]

He is identifying social power as the key to enabling mind control and tellingly identifies six keys to its. When reading them, consider what entity in America possesses all of them.[10]

1. **Coercive** Ability to punish
2. **Reward** Ability to reward
3. **Legitimate** Due to status
4. **Expert** Having expertise & knowledge
5. **Reverent** Being liked & respected
6. **Informative** Having information others do not have[11]

There is little doubt that the *Dark Empire* has exercised a great ability to punish those who disagree with their ideological thrust, and reward those who agree with them. They also appear as a legitimate entity who has great knowledge, expertise, and information others do not have. Also, those they have promoted to the status of "star" lend their status to promote the *new moral order*. Because of the lofty status associated with the *viewing screens,* the *Dark Empire* has checked off each on the above list. And this appears to explain the source of their power over the minds of the masses.

CHAPTER NINE

Witches & Rogues

I n the year 1692, the accusations were flying, and according to the young girls making them, so were witches on "poles" across the frosty winter sky. But that wasn't their only claim. Statements that individuals had sent their "specters" across town to torment them, seeking their signatures in the "devil's book" was sure to bring swift justice to the door of the accused. And as the litany of those targeted grew, so did the need for a special "court" to address the threat of witchcraft that had so suddenly riveted the quiet Puritan town of Salem, Massachusetts. For starters, the accused would be thoroughly checked for the presence of any "witch's marks" on their bodies from which their "familiar" might suck for nourishment. But assuming that clear sign was not found, then a "trial" would be held to determine guilt, and everyone accused was guilty. Concern for the protection of the girls being afflicted by these witches caused judicial details, like the right to council, the right to an appeal, and the right to call defense witnesses to be dispensed with. As a result, the fate of those accused was sealed from the start, effectively granting the group of accusing girls the power to send whomever they wished to Gallows Hill, where a noose would quickly find its way around their neck. And for a brief period of time, with the power of life and death in their young hands, only a few brave souls challenged them, and one of them was John Proctor.[1]

Sometimes it is not enough for a man to mind his own business, stirred within by an injustice his conscience cannot resist opposing, regardless of the cost. And that appears to be the case of John Proctor, who chose to speak out forcefully against the travesty unfolding within his midst. As a successful farmer in the region around Salem, Proctor made it known that he believed the young girls were frauds and liars. He scoffed at the idea of witches flying about on poles and openly spoke out against the accusations and the accusers. After his young servant Mary Warren saw the accusing girls gain attention from their antics and then began experiencing her own afflictions, Proctor threatened to beat her unless she ceased. As a result, her afflictions ceased. Finally, after standing almost alone against the *created reality* of witches flying around, the girls turned their attention against their nemesis, accusing both Proctor and his wife of witchcraft, resulting in their immediate imprisonment. Ultimately for his outspokenness, he would be hanged on August 19, 1692, along with five other "witches" on what would become a memorable New England day. But while imprisoned he would send an impassioned letter to the clergy of Boston, causing them to rediscover their consciences, which ultimately brought an end to the *created reality* of witches.[2]

He had made a difference, a *rogue element* challenging *created reality,* but at the cost of his life. Although that *created reality* long ago seems obvious in hindsight, such is not the case for those caught within one. Like *Drones* unable to break free from an illogical *created reality,* the witchhunters blindly followed the emotional beliefs planted in their minds, leading them to their destructive actions.

As a result, such *rogue elements* pose a real threat to those *creating reality* and must be disposed of in whatever fashion is available according to the times. In the day of witches flying about on poles across the Salem sky, that solution was Gallows Hill. Today, however, other methods are employed to deal with those who bring forth information the *Dark Empire* would rather leave buried out of the reach of the masses. The threat *rogue elements* have presented across time is clear. By pointing out to the masses what should have been obvious from the start, *created reality* slowly begins to fade, thus costing the *Dark Empire* its control over the minds of some that had been *absorbed* into it. As such, in spite of their small numbers, *rogue elements* are a danger to the *Dark Empire* and must be dealt with.

Radio

With the rise of mass communications technology in the first half of twentieth century suddenly within the homes of the masses appeared the voices of people speaking from far away. No longer was it only the words of neighbors and folks in town and on the streets who were heard, but now voices carrying the thoughts of strangers began appearing within the privacy of their dwellings. As those voices began speaking out of boxes within homes, the curiosity of it all quickly captured the imagination of the masses. As a result, every home soon possessed one. And it wasn't long before images on *viewing screens* soon followed those voices. Over the course of time, such voices and images began to take on a personality, eventually establishing a form of relationship with those listening and watching. But it was a relationship that could never become reciprocal, existing only in the minds of the masses.

In the early years, before the time of *viewing screens*, radio was the dominant communications technology. Because in the beginning it was controlled by only a few corporations, it possessed a *centralized* nature that allowed it to *create reality*.[3] Those who fled Martians understood this well. But over the course of time because of the relatively inexpensive nature of radio broadcasting equipment, a multitude of stations appeared across the continent in big cities, as well as in small towns. Like newspapers in the day of de Tocqueville, this eventually led to its *decentralization*. Therefore, its ability to *create reality* ended, and there naturally developed *rogue elements* across the nation, broadcasting information suppressed by the *Dark Empire*. Those *rogue elements* question the *created reality* of the *viewing screens* from multiple perspectives and are willing to probe politicians who embrace the *ideology of control*. They also challenge the *new moral order,* as well as the *new economic order,* with free-for-all type debates where the masses participate. It is true freedom that has naturally settled into a polyglot of beliefs. However, that has not stopped the *Dark Empire* from attaining some influence within this medium by purchasing stations located within major markets, as well as partnering with independents radio stations to supply their "news" reports. But because of its *decentralized* nature, attempts at *ideological cleansing* of this medium are destined to fail.

At present, the most famous *rogue element* on radio is Rush Limbaugh, whose fame spread across the nation by exposing what the *Dark Empire* does not report. Such information typically runs counter to the *creation of reality* carefully crafted to promote the *new moral order* or the *new economic order*, and his audience is large …very large. Some estimates have the number of individuals listening on any given week between 14 and 20 million.[4] Therefore, the size of his audience combined with a willingness to counter *created reality* should guarantee him the wrath of the *Dark Empire*. And true to their nature, they have not disappointed.

Any stumble on the part of a *rogue element* is quickly seized upon not only to criticize them, but to galvanize attempts to remove them from the air. This is because those embracing the *ideology of control*, by their nature, do not tolerate dissent because it weakens control. Those efforts typically involve boycotts of advertisers, which Limbaugh has borne the brunt of. However, when an individual embracing the *ideology of control* experiences a similar verbal slip-up, they are granted a pass. Two separate incidents perfectly exemplify this process. Both Rush Limbaugh, and Ed Schultz of MSNBC *viewing screen* fame, used the same highly negative term to describe different women. The woman Limbaugh attacked was promoting the *new moral order*; the one Schultz attacked was a strong opponent of both the *new moral order* as well as the *new economic order*.[5] Here is what an article on Yahoo! Voices reported concerning the results of a boycott organized against Limbaugh relating to the incident.

> The boycott of Rush Limbaugh's show has already resulted in nine of his sponsors removing ads. By Saturday morning, Legal Zoom, Citrix Success, Heart and Body Extract, Auto Zone, Quicken Loans, Sleep Train, Sleep Number and Oreck removed their ads from The Rush Limbaugh Show.[6]

However, in spite of Ed Schultz using the same negative word to describe a woman whose views he opposed, no boycott of his show was organized. Essentially, although those who organized the boycott against Limbaugh claimed to have done so in defense of women, they apparently felt no such urge when it came to an identical remark from Ed Schultz. And the reason why is simple: Rush Limbaugh opposes the implementation of the *new moral order* as well as the *new economic order*, and Ed Schultz favors it. The claim that the boycott was in defense of women was only a cover for an attack against someone who dissented from the *new order* being imposed. It also provided an opportunity for those susceptible to the ploy to be divided by gender for the purposes of control. But removal of a talk show host from radio has its limits of effectiveness.

Any effort to remove a *rogue element* off one station results in it reappearing on another with much of its audience following from the old station. This is true because often individuals on these *rogue programs* have become personalities who possess a following. Therefore, since they have a following, their audience will follow them, thus defeating efforts to suppress their descent. Additionally under such a scenario, the station attempting to shut down their descent would suffer the sudden loss of audience, which would immediately lessen its value. Given these facts, it is unlikely the *Dark Empire* can control radio.

With many stations in the hands of *rogue elements,* a free flow of information from radio exists within many communities, but they must be found by the listener seeking it. Since radio's *decentralized* nature does not lend itself to come under the control of the *Dark Empire, ideological cleansing* is not possible within its ranks. As a result, a kind of natural ideological equilibrium exists, causing it to be more ideologically representative of society as a whole. This is to be expected within a *decentralized* system and results in the following phenomenon being experienced across the dial from coast to coast. Radio talk shows that run hard against the *new moral order* or the *new economic order* flourish almost everywhere they appear, garnering audiences hungry for real information. But radio shows that embrace the *new order* typically either fail or experience low ratings.[7] Why tune in to hear the *viewing screen* drumbeat on a radio?

It is only within a *closed ideological system,* like that of the *viewing screens,* where the *ideology of control* can engage in *ideological cleansing.* It is this cleansing that has allowed programming contrary to the beliefs of the masses to be sustainable. Virtual monopolies can do that. Because radio has not been *ideologically cleansed,* it is not useable in the effort to impose the *new moral order* on the masses. And it has not been *ideologically cleansed* because it is *decentralized.*

Since it is difficult for the *Dark Empire* to gain control over radio, its *Drones* have been assured that radio talk shows consist of fabrications and lies since they typically cut so hard against the *new order*. This is because as in any free medium for exchanging information, numerous radio talk shows expose information that is being hidden by the *Dark Empire*. However, although radio is an important force for freedom of information, it is a mass communications technology that pales in comparison to the power of the *viewing screens,* which are capable of sending dramatic images accompanied with sound, within the homes of the masses.

Since radio is a *decentralized free speech* medium, there is only one method available for the *Dark Empire* to gain control over it. That method is legislatively. That is to say that the only way to counter such freedom is to impose the *ideology of control* over *rogue elements* by forcing them to allocate air time to those espousing the *new moral order* and the *new economic order.*

Newspapers

Because newspapers have a history of freedom since the earliest days in North America, many have remained free in spite of the large financial elements of those embracing the *ideology of control* taking an interest in them. Such freedom is especially true outside America, where newspaper articles not conforming to *created reality* invariably make their way across the Atlantic through the Internet. For those who access the unending volume of newspaper articles appearing over the Internet, originating from across America and the world, they are the best informed in the land, and completely unable to be *absorbed* into the *created reality* of the *viewing screens.* As such, although the *Dark Empire* has assumed possession over numerous newspapers, forming them into a new ideological and financial empire, there is still enough remaining free that those seeking uncontrolled information can find it.[8]

Newspapers that have aligned with the *Dark Empire* are typically from large media markets where their financial empire comes into play. There is usually an inverse relationship between size of the market and the degree to which information against the *new moral order* or the *new economic order* is allowed to be reported to the masses. Therefore, generally speaking, the larger the market, the more controlled the information will be from the newspaper. In other words, it is more likely it will conform to and not attempt to counter *created reality*. However, within such mega markets, newspapers of lesser reach and audience occasionally spring up in response to major newspapers controlled by the *Dark Empire*. New York City is a prime example of this phenomenon, with many challenging the dominance of *The New York Times*.

Because the ranks of newspapers have not experienced the degree of *ideological cleansing* that *viewing screens* have, a reporter from a large newspaper will occasionally contradict attempts to *create reality*, thus causing them to become a *rogue element*. With those embracing the *ideology of control* seeking a larger and more controlling government apparatus, a revealing event occurred in the winter of 2013 as a federal budget "sequester" was about to automatically begin cutting government spending.[9] Even though the federal budget deficit was running over one trillion dollars a year, any move toward a smaller government is anathema to those seeking control over the masses, and is highly unacceptable. The so-called sequester was the result of a negotiated settlement between the Obama White House and Congressional Republicans during the prior year in an effort to avert a government shutdown.

As a result, the Obama Administration, whose policies to advance the *new economic order* included government control over the nation's health care system, as well as a dramatically larger federal budget, attempted to *create reality* on how the masses should view the approaching cuts. Part of the effort involved *creating reality* that the sequester idea was the fault of those opposing greater government ... the Republicans.[10] But those efforts to *create reality* ran into a legendary reporter who knew the truth and was willing to write about it.

Political parties and politicians of every stripe always try to place blame for problems anywhere but on themselves, and it doesn't appear that tendency will end anytime soon. However, it isn't often that one is caught doing it so definitively while in the process, and by the most unlikely source. Carl Woodward, a newspaper reporter well respected by the *Dark Empire*, wrote an article that contradicted the *created reality* being spread about on the sequester.[11] As a result, he incurred the wrath of the Obama Administration and some within the *Dark Empire*. Having broken the Watergate story in the 1970s, which ultimately led to the resignation of President Nixon, Woodward was viewed as a consummate Washington reporter. So much so, that he was portrayed in a movie concerning the scandal, *All the President's Men*.[12] What added to his mystique within the ranks of the *Dark Empire* was that the president he helped take down had pointed out the ideological purity of those controlling the *viewing screens*. But, apparently, Woodward's desire to inform the masses trumped any thoughts to conform to the message being circulated by the White House that the sequester was the idea of Congressional Republicans. With the exception of FOX News, a *rogue element*, all other *central controllers* of *viewing screens* played along with the effort to place blame elsewhere, their massive news teams appearing to be oblivious to the events that transpired, which brought the sequester about.[13] However, Woodward, who had previously interviewed senior White House sources after the sequester had been negotiated, knew the truth and wrote about it. This from his article in *The Washington Post*:

> Obama personally approved of the plan for Lew and (Rob) Nabors to propose the sequester to Senate Majority Leader Harry Reid ... They did so at 2:30 p.m. July 27, 2011, according to interviews with two senior White House aides who were directly involved.[14]

At that time Jack Lew was the president's Chief of Staff, and Nabors was the White House's chief liaison to Congress. Essentially, the report, which goes as far as to cite the date and even the time it took place, completely contradicted the White House efforts to *create reality* for the masses on the issue. As a result, the response of the White House to the report was swift and furious. According to reports, it involved one of the president's top aides, Gene Sperling, who "shouted at Woodward" during the 30-minute call, then followed it up with an email ending in the words, "You're going to regret this."[15] By reporting as he did, Woodward in that moment went from being a hero of the *Dark Empire*, to a *rogue element,* contradicting *created reality*, and was, therefore, attacked.

After Woodward's report came out indicating that the sequester idea had, in fact, been Obama's idea additional trouble began coming his way. Suddenly, Tanner Colby, writer for a political Internet site associated with *The Washington Post*, found "troubling things" about a book Woodward had previously written.[14] Alex Pareene of the leftist Internet site Salon.com, considered Woodward's words "insane."[17] MSNBC host Ed Schultz thought his actions represented "a total failure by a legendary journalist."[18] The liberal Internet news source Huffington Post, along with John Avlon of CNN, would defend the rough handling of their fellow reporter, indicating it was no big deal.[19] The Woodward incident reflected the intolerance of those embracing the *ideology of control* against any that cross it, no matter who they are. The ultimate impact of the harsh treatment against Woodward was to send a clear message to all who were listening: No matter who you are, do not challenge the *reality being created* on a big issue of the day.

Internet

For the *Dark Empire*, the invention of the Internet presented the potential of a powerful new *rogue element,* one capable of countering *created reality* with nonconforming information delivered directly to the masses. After all, the information and videos accessed from its countless options are broadcast over a monitor, which is a *viewing screen,* possessing as much power over the minds of the masses as those of television. Such an evolution of the Internet would create a new and powerful *decentralized* media, or free press, which by its nature could not conform to anyone's *created reality.* For those embracing the *ideology of control,* such a loss of control is completely unacceptable. Since the evolution of the *Dark Empire* came about through *ideological cleansing,* as indicated by a host of studies, it was their purified ranks that allowed them to guide the masses in a social and economic direction. Such unity through cleansing allowed *creating a reality* that advanced the *new moral order* and the *new economic order.* And without any effective ideological counterweight within their purified ranks, the *imposition of choice through overwhelming influence* became possible. But there was the problem. Any attempts to *ideologically cleanse* the Internet would be impossible, since by its nature it was too easy for information portals to be established. In light of that challenge it is interesting to observe how the Internet has actually evolved, which, coincidentally, resolved the threat.

When it comes to how the Internet has evolved, the headline in *The New York Times* would say it all: "More News, Less Diversity." Although there is a wide array of sources that can be accessed, the reality is that it does not play out that way. As the *Times* article would explain, "It's because Internet traffic follows a winner-take-all pattern that is much more ruthless than people realize." Adding, "Users may be able to choose from millions of sites, but most go to only a few." Although there are a few very successful sites, "the rest remain invisible to the majority of users."[20] And which news sites have won this winner-take-all sweepstakes? Pew Research would answer that question in its annual report on the state of the media in the United States.

As readers migrate to the web, however, one thing has remained remarkably stable: the news organizations Americans turn to.

The traditional players remain the most popular sources for digital news."[21]

Companies that measure online readership would all arrive at the same conclusion of where the overwhelming majority of Internet users would end up for their news.

But all arrive at essentially the same lineup of the biggest sites. Long-standing brands —- newspapers, network news and cable news channels."[22] (Emphasis added)

The word "all" is used to stress the overwhelming dominance of only a few information sources on the Internet being accessed by the masses. Of these "long-standing brands," seven of the top-10 Internet news sites in the United States are owned by the six mega-media corporations that own virtually all other media in the country.[23] The remaining three, although owned by other corporations, are on the left side of the political spectrum, and naturally withhold information that counters the *new moral order* and *new economic order* where they can. And how dominant is their control of Internet news in the United States? Within those top-10 sites, there were 436 million unique users per month out of just 212 million total Internet users (May 2012).[24] That massive overlap indicates that attempts by the user to find different news perspectives brings them right back to another site controlled by a branch of the *Dark Empire*.

But like radio, there are still *rogue elements* that receive some traffic because users specifically seek them, but they have to be sought. And that is where the problem is. The chance of Internet surfers finding a *rogue element* in a search for news is slim. And that is where many of these mega-media sites appear to overwhelm other news outlets. Their sites typically appear on the first page after a person inputs a search term seeking news or information, effectively blocking out *rogue elements*. Therefore, the top ten "conservative" Internet news sites, which report information that counters the *new moral order* and the *new economic order*, have an average ranking of only around 3,055, and the reason for this is simple.[25] The *Dark Empire* long ago saw the potential of the World Wide Web to break its grip on the minds of the masses. Therefore, they used their financial and media empires to extend their tentacles to the computer screen.

As a result, what has happened to the Internet is the same as what has happened to the *viewing screens*, with control over the bulk of what the masses see and hear having become *centralized* into the same few hands that control the *viewing screens*. This *centralization* has allowed them to continue the *manipulation* of the minds of the masses using the same method as with the *viewing screens*: the *imposition of choice through overwhelming influence.* Although it appears as a choice, it really isn't. Essentially, like television, the free speech of the Internet has become a commodity that has been cornered by those powerful enough to do so, careful to *create the reality* of choice without it truly existing. And essentially, for a surfer to locate a *rogue element* they must already know where to specifically find it. This effectively eliminates individuals who do not already know about them. But like the chicken-egg paradox, which comes first, finding these *rogue information* sources to obtain information withheld, or gaining the knowledge being withheld to understand the need to seek them?

Since websites controlled by the *Dark Empire* receive the bulk of news traffic on the Internet, it is apparent they found a way to prevent it from becoming a giant *rouge element*. They simply absorbed it into their media empire, relegating news outlets that present information that counters *created reality* to its backwaters.

Viewing Screens

When it comes to controversy, U.S. presidents are able to create a lot of it. And in line with that maxim, President Obama would be no different. He would order military drone strikes against American citizens overseas suspected of being involved in terrorist activities ... without a trial of any kind to determine guilt. His administration would also indicate that a legal basis existed for such strikes to take place within the United States, shocking civil libertarians and constitutional experts alike.[26] The difficult economy he inherited from President Bush would continue limping along into his second term, becoming his recession and one that appeared to never end.[27] Overseas, although America was not threatened, he would find the need to unleash an undeclared war in Libya, bypassing the constitutional requirement for Congress to approve the action.[28] His efforts to appoint individuals of his choice to various boards would take the form of recess appointments, designed to circumvent the constitutional requirement of Congress to approve such appointments. Those actions would be reversed by an emphatic Supreme Court that would throw them all out.[29] And when the U.S. Ambassador to the newly "liberated" Libya would be gunned down, along with three other Americans, his administration's approach to the tragedy would include grave inconsistencies in their story about what happened, leaving the shadow of dishonesty in its wake.[30] Although all of these events were different in their nature, they all had something in common-the potential to evolve into a serious scandal for any sitting president. But they also had something else in common-they would all be either ignored or significantly underplayed on the *viewing screens*. That is, except for one small *rogue element*.[31]

Consistent with the observation that the *Dark Empire* will protect highly placed political leaders who embrace the *ideology of control*, President Obama would benefit from it to an extent never before seen in modern times.[32] Having pressed an advance of the *new moral order* to include the institution of marriage, and the *new economic order* to consume the health care sector of the economy, he epitomized the desires of those embracing the *ideology of control*. Therefore, a kind of covering, if you will, appeared to be placed about him by those controlling the powerful *view-

ing screens, never allowing the litanies of events to reach their destructive potential. In addition to having found their ideological soul mate, it was as though the *Dark Empire* had another vested interest in protecting him from those events, and, in a sense, they did. In 2008, when then-Senator Obama was campaigning for the presidency, media elites would financially contribute to his campaign by a staggering 20-1 ratio versus his opponent, indicating a degree of commitment that later translated into the protection of him.[33] But their direct financial contributions to his campaign would pale in comparison to in-kind contributions. Following the 2008 presidential election, the nonpartisan "Project for Excellence in Journalism" would conclude that campaign news coverage of Senator John McCain, Obama's opponent, was three times more negative than coverage of Senator Obama.[34] Such negative coverage is used to *create a reality* for the masses, which results in *manipulating* them toward the candidate who supports the *new moral order* and the *new economic order*. Although such a method is subtle, making it difficult for the masses to notice, it is highly effective in shifting a small segment of votes, but enough to affect the outcome of an election.

Although Barack Obama has enjoyed the overwhelming support of the *Dark Empire* throughout his national political career, there has been a fly in the ointment of *created reality* ... a *rogue element* called FOX News. Because FOX is the only *rogue element* reporting on *viewing screens*, it is despised by those embracing the *ideology of control*, and it shows. When union thugs attacked a FOX News reporter covering a protest rally in Michigan, ABC, NBC, and CBS would fail to report it to the masses,[35] and the reason why is clear. By reporting such information to the masses, *rogue elements* receive sympathy, which counters the *created reality* that they are bad. And for much the same reason, they would all but ignore the story of a FOX reporter being sent to jail for protecting her source on a highly sensitive story.[36] Withholding the event from the masses would take place in spite of stories where the "court verses reporter" typically attract major media coverage simply because of their nature. But here too the *Dark Empire* would demonstrate a unified effort to not grant a *rogue element* the credibility that comes from the knowledge that one of their reporters is willing to go to jail to keep the masses informed. It simply contradicts *created reality* too strongly.

Comedians set up by the *Dark Empire* with their own shows would get into the act, frequently making FOX News the brunt of their jokes, always careful to *create the reality* that what the network reports is false.[37] And the Obama White House would lead the charge against the *rogue*. If there is another case of a White House effort to delegitimize a news organization such as experienced by FOX, it is not easily found. It would be the president himself who would single out the news organization as an impediment to progress in Washington.[38] And when the FOX News team were the only ones asking tough questions concerning the killing of the U.S. Ambassador in Libya, the network's reporters would be excluded from the White House briefing calls on the subject.[36] Administration attempts to *create reality* that FOX News is "not really a news station," would come from none other than senior presidential advisors.[39] Anita Dunn, an administration official whose shady past only FOX would delve into, would join the chorus against FOX indicating, "We don't need to pretend that this is the way that a legitimate news organization behave."[40] And others would get into the act as well.

Organizations dedicated to the destruction of FOX would be formed by individuals that embrace the *ideology of control*. One of them, Media Matters, would commit $10 million and 90 staff members to its "war on FOX."[41] Later, in a letter to various organizations that share that goal, after bragging about the Obama White House's efforts to delegitimize FOX, the leader of Media Matters wrote the following.

In recent days, a new level of scrutiny has been directed toward

Fox News, in no small part due to statements from the White House, and from Media Matters, challenging its standing as a news organization.[42]

Usually when an organization is attacked in the manner that FOX has experienced, it is because they have become too powerful. But that is not the case here. The special attention FOX has received has come in spite of possessing a prime-time news audience of only 7.5% of the overall national market.[43, 44] That means that only about one out of every thirteen viewers is tuned in to their news programming, with all of the remaining viewers staring into *viewing screens* controlled by the *Dark Empire*. Therefore, it is not audience level that draws attacks against FOX, but the need for *control of reality*. And since FOX has not conformed to the *created reality* that the *new moral order* and the *new economic order* have been beneficial to society, the actions against it occur as a natural reaction from those embracing the *ideology of control*. This is because those embracing the *ideology of control* always place ideology above freedom, while presenting the *created reality* that they do the opposite.

However, in spite of the existence of FOX the *viewing screens* remain totally dominated by the *Dark Empire*, retaining the ability to withhold information from the masses that counters *created reality*. With its powerful and ideologically purified message sent into the homes of the masses, the *ideology of control* should continue to direct them socially and economically into the future.

Individuals

Like John Proctor long ago, within organizations dominated by those embracing the *ideology of control,* individuals who do not conform are often treated like a *rogue element*. They are victimized for questioning the implementation of the *new moral order,* or any aspect of *created real-*

ity. The treatment of Governor Sarah Palin, who did not conform to the *created reality* of how a woman is supposed to think, demonstrated this phenomenon well. [45, 46, 47, 48, 49] But most often it is not the famous who experience the wrath of being a *rogue*, but individuals whose names and stories are never heard.

However, occasionally such stories do surface, allowing incredulous audiences to see and hear a kind of "John Proctor" incident in their day. One such incident takes us to a classroom at Florida Atlantic University located on the east coast of Florida, where a class titled, "Intercultural Communications," was being taught. Why intercultural communications is important one can only surmise, but it was important for the students in that class to write the name "Jesus" on a piece of paper, place it on the floor, and stomp on it.[50] When one student refused to do it, and after complaining about the "lesson," he ended up being disciplined by the professor who was supported by the university administration.

The lesson associated with the incident involved the importance of "symbols" to people, seeking to ascertain student reactions to a request to "stomp" on an emotionally associated word.[51] The professor of the class, vice chairman of the Palm Beach County Democratic Party, would use an instruction book that specifically offered "Jesus" as the only name to be placed on the paper. It is obvious that a host of other icons could have been used by the author of the manual, but none were. It is also clear that instructors "teaching" their students using the manual could have chosen other icons and accomplished the same effect.[52] But the whole incident raised other questions to ponder. Is it a coincidence that a member of a political party that has a problem placing "God" in its party platform would approve of such an exercise? Is it surprising that a political activist of a political party which embraces the *ideology of control* would be a professor at a university? Is it surprising that the instruction manual would offer only the word "Jesus" to be the one stomped upon? Although the student became a *rogue element* in the moment of refusal, is it surprising he was disciplined for voicing objections to an exercise that so blatantly offended an icon of traditional religious beliefs?

❀   ❀   ❀   ❀   ❀

Because the *Dark Empire* withholds certain information, the existence of *rogue elements* constitutes a threat to its dominion over *Drones*. But it is also the masses at large that are impacted since many use the same "news" sources, rendering them unaware and incapable of running their "democracy." Usually the information withheld would either build a case against some element of the *new moral order* or the *new economic order*, or do real harm to a highly placed political leader sympathetic to the cause of control. As a result, all *Drones* are told that *rogue elements* are not serious news outlets, and some of what they say is simply untrue and nothing more than an effort to sway the masses politically. This approach leaves the *Drone* with the impression that they are better informed than those accessing *rogue elements* for information. This accomplishes several goals. It presents *rogue elements* as irresponsible and even reckless for providing this "false" information. At the same time it *creates reality* that reassures *Drones* of the superiority of their own "news" sources, and thus, themselves, as possessing superior information.

The process of using *Drones* to attack *rogue elements* involves the application of emotionally charged negative *labels* pressed into their minds, directing them toward *meaningful action* against their target. And because emotion is used to *manipulate* them, they lack a consistent response to similar events. In the case of the Rush Limbaugh boycott, those directed against him saw no need to treat a similar offender equally.[53] Such unequal treatment of similar circumstances is a characteristic of the emotionally driven, not the logically driven. Over the course of time, it results in *Drones* experiencing emotional pain associated with information from *rogue elements*, producing a response which effectively inoculates them against considering what is being revealed. The entire effort on the part of the *Dark Empire* to *label rogue elements* is a disinformation campaign to keep the masses away from sources of uncontrolled information.

All of this was easily observable within the 2008 U.S. presidential election where *rogue elements* were attacked for attempting to reveal information about then-Senator Barack Obama. The effort involved attempts to expose past and present associates of his who appeared to be of a questionable nature. In situations like this, the *Dark Empire* will refuse to look into the relationships, and the masses that access them for "news" will simply never hear about it. In the case of Obama, in spite of the list of such individuals being lengthy, it drew no attention from the *centrally controlled viewing screens* with the exception of FOX News. However, within a *decentralized* free press environment there would have been a free-for-all to investigate to see if there was any fire behind the smoke. In such a free press environment the masses are empowered, allowing the chips to fall where they may.[54, 55]

Rogue elements will dig deeply into that which the *Dark Empire* would rather remain unknown to the masses. Occasionally, a *Drone* will experience a situation where individuals accessing *rogue information* appear to be better able to predict future results based on current knowledge, indicating they are better informed. This usually happens when someone they know and trust tells them something that counters the *created reality* they have been *absorbed* into. Since so much information of a significant nature is withheld from the masses via the *viewing screens*, this phenomenon invariably will take place even though the *Drone* will not access *rogue elements*.

Should a *Drone* suddenly begin reading or watching *rogue programming,* then the possibility exists that they will be empowered because free-flowing information empowers the individual and thus creates a plausible scenario wherein a *Drone* could break free from the effects of *absorption*. Therefore, this has resulted in efforts to remove *rogue elements* from the airwaves. This, too, is an observable phenomenon as recorded in the Rush Limbaugh case.[56] As demonstrated in the case of Limbaugh, *Drones* are often made to engage in *meaningful action* against a specific *rogue individual* because some opening against that individual appeared. Perhaps they were involved in a publicly embarrassing incident, or they misspoke in such a way that allowed a created caricature of them to go into full blossom. In those cases, the *Drone* is directed through the utilization of *labeling* to assist in an effort to destroy the *rogue individual* who has suddenly become vulnerable. All *Drones* are directed against an individual or organization through the use of emotionally embedded *labeling*. Since many such *labels* have been pressed within the mind of the average *Drone* with high emotion attached to it, some experience great anger against those *rogue elements*.

Within a decentralized free-press environment, there is no such thing as a *rogue element,* but only competing media outlets willing to report any information to the masses, knowing that if they do not then a multitude of other outlets will. Within the *centrally controlled viewing screens* dominated by an *ideological collective*, that is not the case. Under such an undemocratic system, once a news outlet releases some breakthrough information that undermines the interests of the *ideology of control,* the natural free press hungers to investigate and report it is suppressed by ideology. As such, there is certain information they never release because of the degree of impact it could have on their cause. There is other information that eventually will be released but downplayed in an effort to mitigate its impact on their ideological goals.

Occasionally, efforts to *create reality* take the form of direct deception, and when uncovered, *rogue elements* shine in revealing it. This adds to the tension between *rogue elements* and the *Dark Empire*. One such event took place during a U.S. presidential election.

MANIPULATING MAN

As the masses stared into their *viewing screens,* the evening "news" began with a report on the U.S. presidential campaign in full swing at that time. And that night there was something special to show them. With a little more than a month remaining before the election, a *central controller* of *viewing screens* began showing a video of the presidential candidate Mitt Romney (Republican) speaking at a rally in which he was accompanied by his running mate. And the choice between Romney, a free-enterprise traditional values candidate, and the incumbent, President Barack Obama, could not have been more striking.

As the report streamed across *viewing screens* throughout the nation, it began with the masses seeing a typical campaign setting, with both Mitt Romney and his vice presidential running mate, Paul Ryan, standing on a platform. And then it happened. The masses were informed that instead of the crowd chanting the name of Romney, which would be normal at such a rally, they had shouted the name of his vice presidential candidate, indicating an embarrassing preference for him instead. Then, in a moment that had to make viewers cringe, the presidential candidate began stressing both names on the ticket, apparently chiding the crowd for not mentioning his name. And when the *viewing screen* session was over, the masses believed that an embarrassing moment had taken place on the campaign trail that day.[57]

But sometimes reality crashes the party of those creating it. *Rogue elements* began picking up on the story, and after investigating, soon discovered that, in fact, the crowd had been chanting Romney's name, and not the other way around. It was then out of graciousness he reminded the crowd about his running mate. The entire effort, it seems, was to belittle the candidate opposing the one so supportive of the *new order*. And with the exception of a *rogue element*, FOX News, all other *centrally controlled* networks withheld the scandal from the masses, essentially showing their tacit support of the deception.[58, 59] With their minds steeped in *created reality,* usually when *Drones* are informed about such revelations, the information is treated as rubbish.

The degree of vilification that an individual *rogue element* will experience by the *Dark Empire* is directly proportional to the sum of his audience numbers plus the depth of its resistance against the imposition of *created reality*. That is to say any *rogue element* that possesses a large audience and strongly attacks the *new moral order* or the *new economic order* will be severely vilified through the application of *labels*.

Because highly negative emotions are planted within the minds of *Drones* against *rogue elements*, many of them receive a high number of death threats from *Drones*.[60] Such information is newsworthy within a *decentralized* free-press environment, but within the *Dark Empire's centrally controlled viewing screens*, it is simply withheld from the masses. This is because if disseminated, it would bring sympathy to a *rogue element* and thus counteract the highly negative *created reality* against them.

Had the *viewing screens* been completely *decentralized* upon their introduction in the 1940s, there is little doubt *ideological cleansing* would never have taken place, resulting in the new medium becoming a powerful addition to the free press and further empowering the masses. Under the conditions de Tocqueville observed, such a *decentralized* media would have assured the continuation of democracy within America. Since that did not take place, democracy has receded, being replaced by the ascendency of the *Dark Empire,* whose will is now done.

PART III

Control

CHAPTER TEN

Tyranny!

I t was a turning point in world history, a moment when the unknowable future met the currents of another possible course. It arrived just prior to the commencement of hostilities in what would become known as the Revolutionary War. It was an inflection point where the war might have been avoided with the king and his New World subjects mending their growing rift. Had that happened then, the relationship between them would have continued as it had for the previous one hundred years or so. But had that happened, the United States would never have been born, or its birth would have happened differently and sometime later. But fate has a way of rescuing what is meant to be, injecting itself at the perfect moment and bringing inevitability along with it.

With tensions between the British and colonists growing hotter by the month, an effort at reconciliation in the form of a written message made its way across the Atlantic. Composed by colonial leaders and addressed to King George, it was meant to reassure him of his American subjects' loyalty, carefully placing blame for all difficulties on the king's ministers, not the king. But that document, appropriately named "The Olive Branch Petition,"[1] which was so carefully crafted to bring reconciliation, would ironically provide the spark that lit the fuse, leading to the shot heard around the world. Not only would the king not accept its conciliatory words, but in a great insult, he would refuse to even read it.[2] As a result a war that had been unthinkable only a few years earlier now became inevitable. The next message sent from the colonies to His Majesty would arrive a year later in 1776. But unlike the conciliatory one that proceeded it, this one would be the Declaration of Independence, severing ties and signaling war. However, like all historical moments, this one had its beginnings in a chain of events that began years earlier.

Over the course of time, the British colonies in North America had been allowed to conduct their affairs without much interference from the Crown, representing a time of benign neglect, with the colonists settling into a form of self-regulation. Essentially, they had been free to lead their lives unhindered by substantial dictates from across the sea. However, that would all change in 1754 with the outbreak of a European war between England and France that, inevitably, spread to the New World. The American colonists would fight alongside their British brethren, and victory would come to both in 1763. But the war had emptied the king's treasury, causing him to suddenly look to his colonies for taxes that had never before been pursued. Since their previous relationship to Britain had allowed them great latitude in determining their own affairs, the colonists had felt no particular need for representation within the British Parliament. But suddenly with an assortment of taxes now being levied on them, they wanted to have their voices heard in the halls of government.[3] As their continued efforts for representation were denied and requests upon them from London increased, so did the anger of the colonists.

The refusal of representation within the British Parliament by the king represented what Locke described in his *Two Treatises of Government* as a fundamental violation of the Law of Nature.

> The liberty of man in <u>society is to be under no other legislative power but that established by consent in the commonwealth,</u> nor under the domination of any will, or restraint of any law, but what that legislative shall enact according to the trust put in it.[4] (Emphasis added)

Since the colonists had requested, and were denied their own representatives within parliament, those governing and taxing them began to take on the form of tyranny. Thus the king's refusal of their petitions for representation constituted a fundamental breach in Natural Law, allowing the colonies the Natural Law right to break free from Britain.

It was Locke's political philosophy that laid the foundation for that break which would come in the form of the Declaration of Independence sent by the colonists to the king a year after the "Olive Branch Petition." That declaration spelled out in terms consistent with Locke's writings a series of violations which established that tyranny existed, and therefore so did the natural remedy of the colonists to break free.

In the case of the Revolutionary War, the British argued that the colonists were already being represented through the good will of representatives elected in Britain, and such representation should be good enough. As such, it was asserted that the colonists had a form of virtual representation. That is to say that the case was made by the government in London that since parliament was representing the interests of subjects in all British territories, even though they did not elect their own leaders, that kind of representation should be good enough.[5]

But such reasoning was a clear abridgement of the concept of representation as applied to a free and democratic people. Such reasoning, if applied today, would justify one of the fifty states forgoing representation in Congress on the basis that the remaining forty-nine states would look out for their interests. Although individuals of goodwill within such a legislature might seek the best for the unrepresented state, it would represent a clear abridgement of the theory of representative government. Such an abridgement, although having a vague appearance of representation, would also violate Locke's principle that "the liberty of man in society is to be under no other legislative power but that established by consent in the commonwealth." Upon that foundation rested the break with Britain.

It would be Thomas Jefferson who would acknowledge that Locke's *Second Treatise of Government* "provides the general principles of liberty and the rights of man, in nature and in society...approved by our fellow citizens...."[6] However, it is clear such a foundation, as acted upon in 1776, was not peculiar to that time in history alone, but continued to be a natural right possessed by all into the future indefinitely, allowing the posterity of those same colonists to draw upon it should tyranny rise up in the land again. And this is where the *Dark Empire* comes into consideration, causing the following question to be raised. Does such an unnatural entity have legitimacy within a true democracy, Natural Law, or the document which grew out of it, the United States Constitution?

Decentralization of Power

Tyranny thrives on the *centralization* of power. That is because *centralization* grants it the means of overwhelming any who might seek a course different from its own. And by consuming most or all power within what was meant to be a free system, it prevents others from exercising it, effectively drowning them out in a sea of overwhelming might. It was with this mindset that the Founding Fathers embraced Locke's concept of "separate powers," wherein the government of the United States would have its power divided into three equal parts: Executive, Legislative, and Judicial. But in a broader sense, the act of dividing the government in such a way was to *decentralize* it, creating a wall against tyranny by not allowing an environment that was conducive to the *centralization* of power in the hands of the few. It was as though they were securing the treasure of democracy with a lock that took three different keys, possessed by three individuals and that must be operated simultaneously. Within a *centralized* system there would have been only one.

By establishing separate branches of government, they set up a system where effectively each branch placed a check on the power of the other, thus stifling the rise of despotic forces that appear to naturally develop over the course of time. Additionally, in order to ensure that a sudden concentration of legislative power might not fall under the control of a momentary movement, it was decided to *decentralize* it further by dividing it into two houses, the Senate and the House of Representatives. Then an effort was made to ensure these two legislatures would not be too similar in their perspectives by granting the Senate six-year terms, and the House only two-year terms.[7]

But not satisfied that employing Locke's theory of separate branches to *decentralize* the power of government institutions was enough to safeguard against the rise of tyranny, the Founding Fathers went on to construct a series of rights granted to the people that further diffused power. Their most powerful attempts were contained within the First and Second Amendments to the Constitution. The Second states:

A well regulated militia, being necessary to the security of a free state, the right of the people to keep and bear arms, shall not be infringed.[8]

Referencing the "security of a free state," this amendment is designed for circumstances in which all of the other safeguards against tyranny had failed. In the final analysis, if all else failed to prevent tyranny, then the right to abolish the government would be ensured by a well-armed citizenry. Since each individual was granted the right to bear arms, each represented a highly *decentralized* counter-force against tyranny. This right represented the ultimate *decentralization* of power within the land. It is also a right that by its very nature causes the *ideology of control* to be opposed to it because the right to bear arms empowers the masses. However, since realistically only a grand coming together of such individuals could present an insurmountable obstacle to tyranny, only under egregious circumstances could such a rare event ever take place.

Freedom of the Press

Because there are certain traits common to tyranny, one being the suppression of free-flowing information, the guarantee of a free press contained within the First Amendment was to ensure that an array of watchful eyes would always be cast upon the activities of government, as well as events across the nation, thus providing the masses with the information necessary to govern. In addition to guaranteeing freedom of the press, the First Amendment included the right of free speech, another factor diffusing power to every citizen in an act of grand *decentralization*.

> Congress shall make no law respecting an establishment of religion, or prohibiting the free exercise thereof; or <u>abridging the freedom of speech, or press</u>; or the right of the people peaceably to assemble, and to petition the government for a redress of grievances.[9] (Emphasis added)

Wanting to ensure a truly free press for the sake of the democracy they had just secured, the Founding Fathers made it clear its freedom must not be abridged by Congress in any way. By understanding the meaning of the word "abridge," we see just how significant the concept of a free press was to them. According to Merriam-Webster's Dictionary, the term "abridge" means "to reduce in scope, to diminish, to deprive."

In other words, Congress was never to limit the press in functioning or do anything that would diminish its effectiveness in serving the people. Thomas Jefferson summed up their fears relating to the "abridging" of the freedom of the press in a letter to John Jay in 1786 stating,

> "Our liberty cannot be guarded but by freedom of the press, nor that be limited without danger of losing it."[10]

Jefferson's concern was that anything which could have the effect of limiting the activities of "freedom of the press" created the danger of losing freedom overall. Of course, the media he and the other Founding Fathers observed at the time these words were written was highly *decentralized* and thus without any ability to "establish great currents of opinion that sweep away or overflow the most powerful dykes," as de Tocqueville would later observe. In other words, it could not implant a *new moral order* on the masses within just a few short decades. Having embraced the concept of a *decentralized* government through the dispersion of its power into three separate branches, the free press they saw lined up with that same concept. This effectively left the masses to determine the direction of the nation and rendering the "press" impotent at coming together to reverse that safeguard. Therefore, the masses were free in their minds and free to rule their nation. Years later Jefferson would go even further in a letter, connecting freedom of the press with that of a free mind.

> To preserve the freedom of the human mind...and freedom of the press, every spirit should be ready to devote itself to martyrdom; for as long as we may think as we will and speak as we think, the condition of man will proceed in improvement."[11]

In Jefferson's references to "freedom of the human mind" as well as to the right to "think as we will and speak as we think," he places freedom of the mind at the epicenter of true liberty. But what feeds this freedom of the mind as well as those freedoms that spring forth from it is freedom of information. With freedom of the mind so significant for the realization of true freedom, it stands to reason any force which impairs that freedom would be unacceptable. Since such freedom could never be "abridged" by Congress, then, logically, it should preclude others from doing the same. There is no reason to believe that the Founding Fathers would have granted a pass to any band of ideologues who found a way to *manipulate* the masses using powerful *created reality* simply because a technological advance empowered them to do so. If the government is precluded from "reducing or diminishing" the free flow of information to the masses, then how can it be acceptable for a group of ideologues to do so by gaining control over its most powerful organ through *centralization*? And are we to believe that the Founding Fathers were talking only about the free flow of information, or does the entire concept of the First Amendment strike at a deeper freedom: the freedom of the mind from *manipulation*? For what good does the right of free speech and press avail any if the minds of the masses are *manipulated*? Since freedom of speech infers the right of the individual to freely express their minds' thoughts, then if an overwhelmingly powerful new technology is capable of imposing a new set of beliefs upon those same minds, how can the essence of the right of free speech be exercised? The simple answer is that such a condition of man is worse than the complete elimination of a free press and free speech because it strikes at the very source of both, the human mind.

Possessing and exercising the ability to *absorb* elements of the masses into *created reality* in order to direct them toward a *new moral order* or *meaningful action* is a clear violation of Jefferson's exhortations to "preserve the freedom of the human mind." The ability to *centrally control* the better part of the essence of what constitutes a free press by placing it into a few hands causes it to be limited to exactly that, a few hands. By its nature, *centralization* takes power from the many and places it in the hands of the few. Moving from many to a few is an act of limitation. To put it another way, such an action causes it "to reduce in scope, to diminish, to deprive," perfectly fulfilling the definition of abridging. As Jefferson pointed out, any kind of limiting of the freedom of the press risked losing it. As he further observed, "as long as we may think as we will and speak as we think" the masses would remain free. But have not the powerful *viewing screens* hindered the masses in fulfilling this? As long as the "media" within the nation remained so highly *decentralized,* there was no risk of losing such freedom of the mind. But that changed with the advent of the *centrally controllable viewing screens.*

Because such power as found in the technological breakthrough of the *viewing screens* was not *decentralized* from its earliest beginnings, it has evolved in such a way as to render the right of freedom of the press and speech meaningless on several levels. The first is referenced by Jefferson as "the free right to the unbounded exercise of reason and freedom of opinion," which has been all but eliminated for large groups within the masses-those that have fallen under the *manipulative* control of *created reality,* especially the *Drones.* But beyond *manipulation* such a *centrally controlled* medium has greatly reduced the flow of real information to the masses, with the *ideology of control* carefully withholding certain information and then crafting that which is released in such a way as to not upend whatever or whomever they seek to promote. Such an abridging of the true value of a free press and the democratic process leaves only the appearance of both, rendering them neutered and into a clear state of abridgement. This is possible because of the incredible power the *viewing screens* exert on the minds of the masses, capable of directing them in significant ways never before allowed. It is an influence so powerful it has been successfully used to transform the masses toward a *new moral order-*one that was anathema to their ancestors not many years ago.

Although this breach in preserving "the freedom of the human mind" has its roots in the inevitable advance of technology, technology is not the enemy. The problem is it was allowed to become *centrally con-*

trolled, thus attracting those seeking to impose their beliefs on the masses, and thus causing the *great dichotomy* to appear. Had the *viewing screens* been *decentralized* from the start, its ranks would have never experienced the clearly observable effects of *ideological cleansing.* It would have become a natural polyglot of views as diverse as the nation itself, rendering it incapable of being used to *manipulate* the masses toward a *new moral order.* Such a *decentralized* condition would represent a truly free press. This was what de Tocqueville had observed, noting the complete inability of a free press from directing the masses toward any ideological goal.

> One conceives without difficulty that among so many combatants [newspapers] neither discipline nor unity of action can be established …Newspapers in the United States, therefore, <u>cannot establish great currents of opinion that sweep away or overflow the most powerful dykes.</u>"[12] (Emphasis added)

Such a condition of media within any country, as described by de Tocqueville, renders the masses in control, unable to be *manipulated* and with no ideological group capable of establishing "great currents of opinion." Essentially, a truly free media allows the masses to evolve in a naturally free way. But with such *ideological cleansing* having been successfully accomplished within the ranks of those in control of the powerful *viewing screens*, it has had the effect of drowning out a diversity of beliefs in a sea of overwhelming might, with an observable abridging of both freedom of the press and speech. Considering that since the time the first colonists arrived on the shores of North America, until around the 1950s, the masses generally held to the same moral beliefs; the imposition of the *new moral order* utilizing the *viewing screens* have "establish[ed] great currents of opinion that sweep away…the most powerful dykes." And strikingly, its powerful and *manipulative created reality* has *absorbed* many into it, causing a new man to appear on the scene, the *Drone.*

Since this particular technological breakthrough sits in the living rooms of the masses *creating a reality* many are incapable of resisting, and is able to alter the most basic and foundational human beliefs, by its very nature it is insidious and far too dangerous to be allowed to be *centrally controlled.* By exhibiting such "superpowers" over the minds of the masses, it has allowed the few to enslave the minds of the many. Thus, it has resulted in an abridging of not only the right to free-flowing information, but the right of free thought and belief development, the most basic of human rights. The result of this has been the destruction of democracy and the establishment within the masses of *Drones, absorbed* into a *created reality,* effectively rendering them as slaves of the *Dark Empire.* Unlike the highly *decentralized* "media" that existed in the time of the Founding Fathers and later observed by de Tocqueville, the *centralized* nature of the *viewing screens* appears to have drawn those embracing the *ideology of control* toward it in great numbers. Since its power over the human mind became obvious from the beginning, it naturally caused those embracing that ideology to gravitate toward it. Because such control has also resulted in *manipulation* of the masses, this *great dichotomy* has produced pure tyranny.

In light of the Founding Fathers' strenuous efforts to decentralize power through branches of government, as well as placing certain key rights in the hands of the people, it is obvious that the concentration of power, such as assembled by this *Dark Empire* was something they feared most. When considering the "superpowers" over the minds of the masses, which those controlling the *viewing screens* brag of possessing, there is little doubt that its *centralization* represents a violation of the intent of the First Amendment, which guaranteed the free flow of information. But its most dangerous characteristic has been its ability to *manipulate* the masses. Such *manipulation* is a characteristic of tyranny.

Jefferson's letter to Roger Weightman, if it is anything, is a warning against such *manipulation* that upends freedom of the human mind and is worth reciting again.

"The Signal of arousing men to burst the chains, under which monkish ignorance and superstition had persuaded them to bind themselves ...restores the free right to the unbounded exercise of reason and freedom of opinion. All eyes are opened, or opening to the rights of man.[13]

Here, too, Jefferson strikes at the heart of the entire reason for the First Amendment, so the "unbounded exercise of reason" could be exercised by all in the land. For without such ability, how else can the masses rule the land? And are not such "chains" of "monkish ignorance" reappearing, enabled by technology? Has not such "monkish ignorance" returned via the *viewing screens,* as evidenced by today's *Drones*?

Ideological Succession

There is yet another aspect of the *Dark Empire* that strikes a shrill chord in this band of tyranny, and was best expressed in January 1776 by patriot leader Thomas Paine. Writing in his booklet titled "Common Sense," he made the case that hereditary succession of power by its very nature was tyrannical. In his day, this grievance was cited against King George since he had come from a long list of monarchs before him, each handing power down to the next in line within their immediate family and effectively circumventing the Law of Nature. Therefore, even in the event that the colonists would gain representation within the British Parliament, the entire concept of kingship represented an additional element of despotism that Locke's words provided the general philosophical reason to oppose. However, it would be Paine who would provide the more specific indictment of the hereditary succession of power.

To the evil of monarchy we have added that of hereditary succession; and as the first is a degradation and lessening of ourselves, so the second, claimed as a matter of right, is an insult and imposition on posterity. For all men being originally equals, no one by birth could have a right to set up his own family in perpetual preference to all others forever, and tho' himself might deserve some decent degree of honours of his contemporaries, yet his descendants might be far too unworthy to inherit them. One of the strongest natural proofs of the folly of hereditary right in Kings, is that nature disapproves it, otherwise she would not so frequently turn it into ridicule, by giving an ASS FOR A LION.[14] (Emphasis part of the original text)

It is understood that kings prefer to be viewed by those under them as lions among men, thus presenting the façade of superiority in an attempt to grant themselves legitimacy to rule. But as Paine so aptly writes, often such succession instead results in an ASS finding its way to the throne, placing the spotlight of nature's disapproval on the whole affair. And since the people have no say in who would ascend to the seat of power, their fate was dictated by the whims of those next in line, whether for good or evil. But Paine's complaint went beyond questioning the right of kings to rule and included the entire structure of aristocracy represented by the ruling Peers in his day, who by right of birth were automatically granted a form of power within the ruling hierarchy. To Paine, both king and aristocracy were illegitimate.

Such hereditary succession of power to rule the masses was a violation of the Laws of Nature because by its nature, the best and most talented individuals could not rise to the top as they would naturally do so within nature. This was because natural attributes were not taken into consideration-only the family tree. If hereditary succession was in line with the Laws of Nature, then a LION would always find itself on the throne, instead of the frequent ASS.

But just as the concept of hereditary succession is anathema to the Laws of Nature, so it is with the method used by the *Dark Empire* to ensure the continuity and homogeneous nature of its ruling elite. Although in this case power is not handed down through the process of hereditary succession, the actual process used is not much different from that abysmal and tyrannical system. With ideology the essential qualification for entry into its ruling circles, it is a *closed ideological system*. A *closed ideological system*, by its nature, is a form of *ideological succession* that violates the same principles of the Law of Nature as does the system of hereditary succession. This is true because it eliminates the ability of individuals to ascend to the upper echelons of its power structure on the basis of natural ability and instead mandates they be a part of the ideological family of the *ideology of control*. They must embrace the *new moral order* as well as the *new economic order* in order to qualify for ascension into its inner circle of power, and therefore it represents a form of *ideological aristocracy*. With the *Dark Empire's* observable success in securing the ideological purity of its ranks and possessing great power over the masses, it has set itself apart from the rest of the nation, making itself into an elite ruling power, or aristocracy, open only to those who fall in line with its ideological thrust. Therefore, for this reason also, those who control the *viewing screens* represent a form of aristocracy and tyranny.

It is also an observable phenomenon that those who have risen to the top of the *Dark Empire's* power structure have ignored the disastrous results of what they have promoted, marking themselves as the ASS, instead of the LION. But they have also demonstrated no remorse for being a part of the destruction of what had previously been a *decentralized* free press, thus lacking justification to rule on a moral level as well.

Natural Law

Fundamental to the Law of Nature, as described by Locke, within the ranks of mankind none are to be subordinate to others, but are equals for the reason that men are "all the workmanship of one omnipotent and infinitely wise maker."[15] Such equality is further knitted together by the fact that each man possesses reason and free will, and therefore being cognitively independent they are therefore inherently independent on a political level as well. As a result, the only form of government that nature justifies is one wherein there is agreement among individuals coming together to freely form it. Such an agreement was to be implemented through a governing structure of *decentralized* power, described by Locke in some detail. That government was centered on his three ruling branches, which the Founding Fathers incorporated within the constitution. This *decentralization* of government power was their effort to ensure that the masses would maintain control. Therefore, the U.S. Constitution is a representation of Locke's political philosophy becoming reality, and as such validates the entire Law of Nature he described, and therefore acknowledges it as the source of its origin. Therefore, because the Law of Nature was antecedent to it, the U.S. Constitution's existence is owed to it. To deny the Law of Nature, is to deny the foundation of the U.S. Constitution.

So having laid out the premise of what made men equal and then carefully detailing the best form of government to accomplish this government of equals, it was necessary for Locke to describe from where and in what form a breach could come against it. Since the Law of Nature is based on mutual respect among men toward one another, he describes why a breach against it is so significant.

> In transgressing the law of Nature, the offender declares himself to live by another rule than that of reason and common equity, which is the measure God has set to the actions of men for their mutual security ...[16]

By describing offenders against the Law of Nature as living by a rule other than that of "reason and common equity," Locke then describes them to be in a fundamental conflict with a system he believes God has established for the benefit of mankind. Therefore, logically flowing from such a train of thought were these words:

> The liberty of man in society is to be under no other legislative power but that established by consent in the commonwealth, <u>nor under the domination of any will</u>, or restraint of any law, but what that legislative shall enact according to the trust put in it.[17] (Emphasis added)

Here it is stated that because such equity among men naturally results in rule "established by consent in the commonwealth," it therefore rules out justifying any force or group of individuals placing the masses "under the domination of any will"[18] outside of such legislative power. Since the *Dark Empire* has demonstrated great power over the minds of the masses, accomplished in unity of purpose through the process of *ideologically cleansing* their ranks, such power, combined with the *central controlling* of the *viewing screens,* creates a system that runs against "reason and common equity." Being an entity with the power to control and *manipulate* the masses, even capable of replacing deeply rooted moral belief systems with a *new moral order*, it qualifies as having placed them "under the domination of [its] will"[19] without being granted such authority. Here, too, it is tyranny. But there is more.

Because the *Dark Empire* is a *closed ideological system* which is the natural result of the process of *ideological cleansing*, there is no ideological counter-weight within it which results in a natural diffusion of power that creates moderation and the consideration of other perspectives as occurs naturally within society. This makes it unlike a society where there naturally exists an array of ideologies testing each other and having the effect of moderation as a form of natural checks and balances. Because through *ideological cleansing* it has no natural counter force within, it is therefore a form of absolute and arbitrary power, capable of moving a segment of the masses in any direction it desires. Such a powerful entity was addressed by Locke in these terms.

This freedom from absolute, arbitrary power is so necessary to, and closely joined with man's preservation, that he cannot part with it but by what forfeits his preservation and life together. For a man, not having the power of his own life, cannot by compact or his own consent enslave himself to any one, nor put himself under the absolute, arbitrary power of another ...[20]

Elsewhere in his *Second Treaties of Government,* Locke described such an entity exercising this form of absolute power as being in a state of war against the basic rights of man. Such absolute and arbitrary power to *manipulate* the minds of the masses toward a *new moral order* as well as *meaningful action* as demonstrated by the *ideological aristocracy* of the *Dark Empire,* cannot be approved by the Law of Nature because according to Locke, man ...

cannot by compact or his own consent enslave himself to any one, nor put himself under the absolute, arbitrary power of another.

As a result, man is not capable of granting such power, as exercised by this *ideological aristocracy* since he cannot consent to his own enslavement. Since its existence is contrary to the Law of Nature, it therefore represents tyranny. Put another way, such ideological power as concentrated within the *centrally controlled viewing screens* has no right to exist under Natural Law, which is the foundation of the U.S. Constitution. Locke was even more specific when it came to such tyranny, describing it in terms that clearly fit the collective actions of the *Dark Empire* within America.

... tyranny is the exercise of power beyond right, which nobody can have a right to; and this is making use of the power any one has in his hands, not for the good of those who are under it. But for his own private, separate advantage. When the governor, however entitled, makes not the law, but his will... [for] the satisfaction of his own ambition, revenge, covetousness, or any other irregular passion.[21]

Since all true freedom has its beginnings in the mind of man, anything that inhibits that freedom is a "power beyond right,"[22] since it counters the most basic and fundamental human rights of man. As such, by having moved a large segment of the masses toward its *new moral order,* it has demonstrated a power that is "beyond right, which nobody can have a right to."[23]

To believe an entity such as the *Dark Empire* is the result of the natural evolution of a free press and therefore somehow acceptable within a democracy, Natural Law, or the U.S. Constitution is to assume that the concept of a free press was never intended for the benefit of the masses, but exists as a commodity for the taking by any entity powerful enough to accomplish the task. Therefore, it means that such freedom of the press can be abridged by any crafty enough or powerful enough to find a means to accomplish such a feat. It also implies a fig leaf of credibility to those despotic forces in modern times which, through less subtle means, assumed control over their nation's "media," placing them in a position to direct the masses by *creating a reality*. It also means that the Nazis, who crafted the term *"create a reality"* after they saw the power contained within the powerful *viewing screen* technology, were on to something that is approved within the Law of Nature. It also places the advance of an ideology above the concept of freedom and completely defies the notion that freedom of the press was meant for the benefit of the masses at large, instead of the exclusive rights of a particular ideological group that united to control it. Therefore, one must decide if such freedom is a right of man or a commodity to be cornered.

If because of its *centralized* nature it was inevitable that some ideology was to gain control over the new technology of the *viewing screens,* then the ideology where the least harm would befall the masses would be those embracing the concept of freedom above control. But since such individuals by their nature do not seek to control, they naturally did not gravitate toward such control. Since those embracing the *ideology of control* appear to possess an insatiable appetite for controlling others, it was only natural they would be the ones who gravitated toward the *viewing screen* industry with an eye on control. Because they embrace the *new moral order* that they have promoted, the flexible morals contained within it allowed them to *ideologically cleanse* their ranks without suffering any moral stress from that action. As a result, a new *force of order* was born that naturally aligned with government, altering the carefully crafted checks and balances designed to prevent tyranny.

As a result of all that has been written within these pages, it is clear that there exists only one solution to effectively deal with this tyranny in order to restore a democracy where the masses once again rule.

CHAPTER ELEVEN

Achilles

I n the mist and shadows of ancient Greek mythology a mother walks toward the bank of a river carrying her newborn son. She is in a hurry and he is scantily clad, and for good reason. It was years earlier the fore-thinker Prometheus had warned the god Zeus that the beautiful woman Thetis, whose hand in marriage he sought, would bear a son who would ultimately become greater than his father. Upon hearing the dire threat against his pride, Zeus gave up on the desire of his heart, she to marry another. Now as she reaches the banks of the river Styx, it is time to fulfill the prophecy of the child.[1]

Like all newborns, he is tiny and weak, but his mother would soon put an end to that. Knowing that all parts of his body doused by the waters would become invincible to the sword, she places his entirety within it, save for the small part where she carefully holds him in by. And when he is removed from the depths, the deed is done. However, it had been more than just a baptism, but a birth, in a sense, that would ultimately produce the greatest warrior the world would ever see. The baby is Achilles.[2]

Then, as the sands of time made their inevitable way into the future, the baby became a man who held the sword better than any before him. And ultimately his path in life took him to the beaches before the grand city of Troy, with its towers and walls impregnable to invaders such as himself. But after ten frustrating years of attempting to breach the fabled barrier, constructed to protect the freedom of the Trojans, Achilles and his fellow Greeks devised a method to finally achieve it. Since direct attacks against the walls were repeatedly repulsed by the free and the brave within, their scheme is to have the Trojans themselves bring them inside. And, unwittingly, Troy falls prey to this masterpiece of deception.[3]

It is a gift, of all things, and that of a horse built of wood and quite large. Entranced by the entertainment of it all, the Trojans allow it within their walls to muse and revel at. And in the evening when the guardians of freedom slept, Achilles and his best warriors, who had hidden within the horse, slipped out and opened the gates of the city to its destruction. But ultimately, Achilles would not share in the victory of the Greeks, with an arrow piercing his heel, the same one where so long ago his mother had held him by. And he died.[4]

❖ ❖ ❖ ❖ ❖

In the time when the masses enjoyed true democracy born of a free press and speech, the walls protecting that freedom were sturdy and high, unable to be scaled by those seeking to control them. For the longest time every assault was repulsed, with freedom secured. But the inevitable advance of technology tends to change things, often bringing forth the *great dichotomy* with it. And so it was with the *viewing screens*, its *centralization* allowing those who sought to control the masses to finally violate the walls of freedom and democracy.

Some will justify this *centralization* by calling it freedom of the press, ignoring the history of a truly free press that existed before the time of *centrally controlled viewing screens*. This was the time when the press had no ability to "establish great currents of opinion that sweep away or overflow the most powerful dykes," as observed by de Tocqueville. But if *centrally controlled viewing screens* are to be considered "freedom of the press," where technology has enabled colluding ideologues to impose their will over the masses, then it implies that the First Amendment was never intended for the benefit of those same masses. It further implies that freedom of the press is a commodity available for small groups to consume using advanced technology. It is the *great dichotomy*. And with the concentration of control over the better part of the powerful *viewing screens* in the hands of an *ideological collective*, any justification granted these tyrants gives an excuse for morphing freedom into control and calling it freedom. And it strikes the paradoxical pose that those turning freedom into control are, simply, exercising their freedom. Thus, the advent of *viewing screens* provided those seeking to control the masses their Trojan horse, brought within the walls of freedom by those they sought to control.

And does not this *centralization* of the *viewing screens* resemble the condition of concentrated economic power that years ago was found to be so antithetical to the essence of free enterprise? Was it not broken up to restore a balance of freedom that served the masses, instead of the few who combined their efforts to control it? To allow such *centralization* within a democracy, one must embrace the belief that freedom is a commodity allowed to be cornered and monopolized by any capable of so doing. That it is a commodity like gold and silver capable of being *manipulated*. Considering the history of anti-monopoly, anti-trust, and anti-racketeering legislation within the United States, designed to avoid a concentration of economic power within the hands of the few, is not free speech and press even more important?

MANIPULATING MAN

The essence of economic tyranny is the concentration of its most precious commodity, wealth, into the hands of the few. And that concentration was one of the reasons the ancestors fled the Old World for the New, where such tyranny had not yet reached its virgin shores. But with the advances in technology that led to the industrial revolution, many workers experienced virtual slave-like conditions in its early days. And those seeking to impose economic chains over the free and the brave came close to accomplishing the task. It was another *great dichotomy,* with the advent of industrial mechanical technology enhancing the lives of some, and resulting in factories that enslaved others, especially the children. But before the dark deed could be completed, the cause of freedom prevailed with anti-monopoly laws breaking apart such *centralized* industrial power in the hands of the few. And this timely action preserved the essence of free enterprise, preventing the growth of a form of economic aristocracy within the New World.

Not long after such economic freedom was secured the inevitable advance of technology marched the nation toward powerful communication systems where voices suddenly began appearing within the homes of the masses. With it the next concentration of anti-democratic forces began to collect within the nation's walls, seeking control and dominion. As the technology of the *viewing screens* allowed free speech and press to become concentrated within the hands of the few, a new form of *ideological aristocracy* evolved. And its ascendency was not unlike that of hereditary succession. But unlike those in olden days who were limited to brute force in their efforts to control and direct the masses, this new *ideological aristocracy* sought and gained control over the minds of many. And they began *manipulating man.*

Therefore, do not the masses possess the same vital interest in disbanding this concentration of power in the hands of the few, just as it did long ago with those seeking to economically enslave them? Is it not as beneficial to the masses now as it was then? Or do some embrace a form of Stockholm syndrome, growing comfortable being told how to think, and see, and hear our times? Such a syndrome appears to develop, over the course of time, where those taken captive begin to bond toward their captors, often to the point of defending them.[5] If so, then what have they become if not *Drones*?

And now the day approaches where *created reality* will grow ever stronger, with holograms soon to begin appearing within the homes of the masses. Such technology will advance *created reality* to a new level of *absorptive* power, finally bringing under control many who had previously resisted. In that day, the darkened ranks of the *Drones* will swell, adding more legions to be directed at the will of the *Dark Empire* toward *meaningful action*. And, therefore, the question arises as to where such power in the hands of the few is ultimately heading?

No Final Destination

The ultimate purpose of the *new moral order* is to replace the rigid moral and religious beliefs handed down from the nation's ancestors with more flexible ones that allow *manipulation* and control. This was necessary since those rigid beliefs created an impenetrable barrier against despotism, as noted by de Tocqueville. In his travels across the continent that would ultimately lead him to write his seminal book, he would place such sturdy beliefs as more important than the laws of the land in ensuring the continuation of democracy. He would also note those beliefs as even more important than the protection of two oceans, which prevented an aggressive enemy on America's borders. His observations would further confirm a host of statements given years earlier from numerous Founding Fathers who viewed those same religious morals as critical to maintaining democracy. But all of that would change with the *great dichotomy*, wherein the technological advance of *centrally controlled viewing screens* would effectively end the *decentralized* free press that had flourished since the time of Plymouth Plantation. And with the amazing success that the *ideology of control* has experienced in pressing its *new moral order* into the minds of the masses, the natural question arises as to what the ultimate destination of the masses is within this *new order*.

As discussed earlier, since the *Dark Empire* is a *closed ideological system,* it possesses no ideological counterweight within itself as is naturally found within society. That is to say within any *open ideological system,* such as is randomly found within society, there is in existence a variety of beliefs acting as a natural counterweight against each other in preventing extremism. However, because of its success in *ideologically cleansing* their ranks, the *Dark Empire* has become a *closed ideological system* possessing no such counterweight toward moderation. Since this *closed ideological system* abhors any absolute moral concept that might regulate behavior, there is nothing to prevent it from entering the *extremist's spiral* wherever greater depths are reached. This means that with no form of ideological counterweight present, it should, therefore, spawn ever-increasing extremes as it pushes its latest version of the *new moral order*. This is confirmed by the easily observable phenomenon of the *new moral order* continuing to reach ever-increasing extremes in each successive decade since the 1950s. However, there is another phenomenon associated with this type of system.

Since such a *closed ideological system* naturally results in the *extremist's spiral*, the *new moral order* can never arrive at a final destination. It can't, because it has none. That is to say there is not in existence any ultimate goal that will satisfy the aggregate of those embracing the *ideology of control,* and pushing the *new moral order*. This is because each new generation coming into the *Dark Empire* is more extreme than those that came before them. This happens because they experience a moral starting point in their youth that was more extreme than the generation before them, and thus causing them to see any effort to take the *new moral order* to a new depth as only a small step. Also, only by pushing the *new moral order* to a greater depth can they see their generation as leaving its mark on the masses.

Since within all movements there is reminiscing about past battles that helped move the cause forward, this produces a desire within the latest generation to accomplish the same. And the only way to accomplish this is to plumb a little deeper. As such the depths of the new morals pressed by those who control the *viewing screens* of today will pale in comparison to those who will come after them. Having no fixed goal means success can never be declared, regardless of what moral depths are plumbed. Therefore, theoretically, even if all traditional moral and religious beliefs are eventually purged from the masses, such a *closed ideological system* would then begin feeding upon itself. At that point, what would constitute a *rogue element* would be those who embraced the old *new moral order*, but cannot bring themselves to embrace some latest advance which even they feel repulsed by.

The Achilles Heel

But as with the ancient myth of Achilles, wherein there existed a spot of vulnerability within his seemingly invincible body, here, too, the *Dark Empire* possesses one. Tyranny strives to create the appearance that what it does is normal and acceptable, thus granting itself a form of legitimacy. But although such "legitimacy" through *created reality* appears to be a mile wide, it is, in reality, only an inch deep. Evidence of this is recorded in the epic level of distrust registered by the unconquered masses, many of whom reject and are repulsed by the *created reality* presented through the *viewing screens*.[6] With the exception of the *Drones*, many within the masses innately know that what presents itself today as a free press is incomparably less so than what existed before the *centrally con-*

trolled viewing screens appeared. And although the ranks of the *Drones* have grown significantly in recent years, especially among the young, the *Dark Empire's* vulnerability can be summed up in the following words:

Spreading the Truth

It is spreading the truth that only a decentralized media represents a free press. Anything else is only the created reality of such.

It is spreading the truth that without such a free press no true democracy can exist, only the façade of one.

It is spreading the truth that such concentrated power, as found within centrally controlled viewing screens, violates Natural Law and represents tyranny.

With *spreading these truths,* the enlightenment of the masses will grow, filling their hearts and minds with a pathway toward restoring the freedom and democracy that once was. The solution for the restoration of a free press and true democracy can be accomplished by one simple action. This action will inevitably lead to the collapse of the *Dark Empire*, and also its *new moral order*. It will restore a free press, one incapable of pressing an ideological agenda. And also will restore a true democracy, one where the masses once again rule. Here, too, it can be summed up:

Decentralization

The media segments of the six giant media corporations must be broken up into a hundred parts with no common ownership allowed.

Therefore, their Achilles heel is *spreading the truth* that brings about the restoration of a free press and the *Dark Empire's* demise through *decentralization.* Such an action would not only lead to the restoration of a free press, but inevitably lead to the breakdown of their *new moral order.* This is because its tenets are unnatural and exist solely because a powerful force continuously promotes it. Because if they "don't promote it, it stays underground," according to the former network president.[7] Without a powerful force united in pressing it upon the masses, such an unnatural set of beliefs, over the course of time, will slowly dissipate resulting in the restoration of dignity and freedom for man. It will also result in rebuilding the walls of freedom that place the masses in control, throwing off the yoke of *manipulation* by an *ideological aristocracy* that is nothing less than tyranny. Because the resulting parts of such a breakup would retain the effects of *ideological cleansing*, each should be sold off through a lottery system, designed to remove the advantage of the powerful and prevent collusion. The resulting break in the yoke of control will guarantee the return of a free media, as in days past, with the natural effect of restoring a democracy where the masses once again rule. And the rebuilding of such walls will "preserve the, freedom of the human mind"[8] for centuries to come because it will establish the following:

A Template

A template for future generations on decentralizing mass communications technology yet to be invented, and as powerful as the viewing screens, before tyranny gains a foothold in their time.

And possessing this understanding that the *decentralization* of powerful communications technology, like the *viewing screens*, is critical for a truly free press to exist, then such an understanding will provide future generations' protection from those seeking to control and *manipulate* them. Without such an understanding, they will almost certainly face a similar threat to what exists today.

✻ ✻ ✻ ✻ ✻

The year was 1776, and writing about the tyranny that existed in his day, Thomas Paine would observe the initial reaction of the masses toward his bold words penned against the British Empire. At the time his words were written, most in the land accepted the notion that the Empire was supreme and a force which one did not challenge. So as Paine and others wrote words that stood up to its tyranny, initially, many had difficulty accepting their challenge. However, over the course of time, and after the yoke of that tyranny was exposed, the truthfulness of those words appeared obvious. But initially some within the land had difficulty in seeing clearly what was destined to become obvious. And as such, Paine would make the following observation concerning his fellow countrymen's initial reaction to his writings.

> Perhaps the sentiments contained in the following pages, are not YET sufficiently fashionable to procure them general favor; a long habit of not thinking a thing WRONG, gives it a superficial appearance of being RIGHT, and raises at first a formidable outcry in defense of custom.[9] (Emphasis part of original text)

And, indeed, to many individuals these monoliths that control the *viewing screens,* and have done so for a length of time, the habit of not thinking such *centralized control* WRONG has given it an appearance of being RIGHT. And, therefore, those embracing this as normal will, at first glance, produce a "formidable outcry in defense of custom"[10] against the thoughts presented herein. But with the passage of time, and as this concept of tyranny stirs, clarity usually comes to those disposed toward freedom. And then the desire for a truly free press overcomes custom.

However, there are others who will find it impossible to ever challenge this tyranny, having traded freedom of the mind for entertainment, and growing comfortable being told how to think. Having become completely *absorbed* into *created reality*, these *Drones* are willing to indefinitely bow the knee of submission. And it is important to note a truth concerning such individuals: They have never advanced the cause of freedom in world history ... ever. Nor do they understand that Natural Law, meaning nature, condemns the current system to that of tyranny because it violates the natural state, which is necessary for a true democracy to exist.

Everything possesses a natural state necessary to sustain its existence. An example of this is man's need for the proper atmospheric conditions to surround him, without which his body cannot continue to survive. He can artificially create such an atmosphere by technologically creating what is necessary. But that takes much to do and certainly does not represent the natural state wherein he thrives. Another example is that of a collection of small goldfish, confined within the glass walls of the *created reality* of where they originally came from, the seas. True, with constant attention they can survive, but only at the behest of their benefactor who feeds them when he chooses. However, this environment pales in comparison to the natural state wherein they thrive. And so it is with that of a free press necessary for democracy to exist.

The natural state of a free press is a highly *decentralized* one. This is true because otherwise it becomes possible for those so inclined to "establish great currents of opinion that sweep away or overflow the most powerful dykes,"[11] which defines control, not freedom. Within a free press natural state, everything is reported, and the ability to withhold information and *manipulate* the masses, does not exist. Freedom from *manipulation* is, of all things, freedom. And since freedom begets freedom it is a natural outgrowth of a free press, which is a natural outgrowth of a *decentralized* press. Thus, a *decentralized* media represents the natural state of a free press because it is antecedent to all resulting freedom thereafter.

As a result, those same masses are empowered with those seeking to control them emasculated. Such a *decentralized* environment not only ensures a free press, but a vibrant democracy. This is because a true democracy, where the masses rule, cannot exist without a free press. However, the natural state of a free press is different from the state of media within tyranny, even one shrouded in all the trappings of a democracy. Within tyranny, media power is concentrated within the hands of a relatively few individuals, empowering them at the expense of the masses. And within such an environment, a true democracy cannot exist, only the carefully created appearance of one.

There are two clear signs present when the natural state of a free press no longer exists within a "democracy." One is the tendency for colluding ideologues to be able to "establish great currents of opinion that sweep away or overflow the most powerful dykes."[12] The other is when those that report the "news" become celebrities in their own right. Such a phenomenon of fame should not take place within a free press natural state because it is too *decentralized,* and, thus, should not produce national celebrities out of "news" people.

In order to restore the natural state for a free press, and true democracy, all *viewing screen* monoliths must be broken up into tiny parts under a form of anti-monopoly legislation, with no common ownership between the parts allowed. And that is also to say there must be no type of cross-ownership allowed, which strongly infers a lottery system for the sale of their parts designed to prevent the old tyranny from retaining control. Thereafter, any actions on the part of individuals or corporations to circumvent this freedom should face a form of anti-racketeering charges. This will return the nation's media, once again, to the natural state of a free press where no ideology will ever again be capable of monopolizing control and *manipulating man.* It will also end the abridgment of free speech and press that began with the advent of *viewing screen* technology. And the *great dichotomy* will finally come to an end.

No true democracy where the masses rule can be sustained against such *centralized* power in the hands of the few. This *decentralization* will result in the masses once again being in control of their society, with the press placed back in the position of reporter, fulfilling the dreams of the

Founding Fathers, and enhancing the "unbounded exercise of reason and freedom of opinion." No longer will the powerful *viewing screens* be able to "establish great currents of opinion that sweep away or overflow the most powerful dykes." And since technology is not the enemy of freedom, but those seeking to control it, such an action strikes a natural balance that allows the masses to enjoy the full benefits of technological advances, without the *great dichotomy* bringing tyranny along with it. And a return to true democracy and freedom will be the result.

Two Futures

On that day long ago when "The Olive Branch Petition" was presented to the British Empire, the masses in North America found themselves at a historical crossroads with the following question before them: remain under British control, or be free? And now some two hundred years later a similar question presents itself. Remain under the yoke of the *Dark Empire* or be free? The continuation of the current path is one where the minds of the masses are destined to be increasingly *manipulated* by this *ideological aristocracy,* which appears bent on controlling virtually every aspect of their lives. And it appears that further advances in technology will likely increase control because of its current *centralized* state. Under such conditions, growing segments of the masses will be directed toward *meaningful action* that serves the ideological goals of this *Dark Empire.* Such *Drones,* unaware of the *manipulation* that possesses them, will live out their lives as tools in the hands of tyranny, their minds carefully crafted to embrace the *created reality* surrounding them.

Additionally, under the current course, the *new moral order* will continue to plumb lower depths, bringing with it all the attendant despair and destruction visible during the first several decades of its implementation. Under such conditions, the family unit will become less and less viable, children suffering the most. The chains of monkish ignorance now observable in so many, lacking any semblance of common sense, will only grow. And those of "higher" education do not appear immune to this affliction. Eventually the point will be reached where the number of those with understanding will become dwarfed by the growing multitude of *Drones*. At that point the "Dark Age" spoken of by Churchill will become the new condition of mankind, enabled by the advances of "perverted science" just as he had warned. Within this all-encompassing darkness, the ability of "restoring the right to the unbounded exercise of reason and freedom of opinion"[13] will end.

When the first settlers arrived on the shores of North America, it was the beginning of an *age of freedom* unlike any which mankind had ever before experienced. With no aristocracy present in this New World to exercise control, freedom prospered. But that age experienced an abrupt end in the middle of the 1700s, with dictates from across the sea beginning to take on the form of tyranny. And the resulting war not much later that threw off that tyranny re-established another *age of freedom* that was to endure into the middle of the 1900s. But history has a habit of repeating itself, and often in the most unpleasant ways. With the evolution of the *great dichotomy,* a new *age of tyranny* was allowed back into the land, empowered by *centrally controllable* technology that effectively ended the *decentralized* free press that had thrived for hundreds of years. And so here the matter rests.

But there is another *age of freedom* possible if enough are roused from their slumber. And it is a future where the ASS, who made its way to an illegitimate throne of its power, is replaced with the LION of freedom. Under such a future, the masses will, once again, rule their nation like the masters of a great ship, limited only by their wills. Under such freedom, the free flow of information will be the norm again, and great issues of the day will have a light of knowledge shone on them, allowing a resolution. It is a condition of freedom where political leaders have no place to hide their incompetence, with the light of exposure constantly shining on them regardless of their ideology. It is a time when none fear being negatively labeled because they spoke their mind. It is a free-for-all environment of freedom because true freedom is a messy affair. And the divisions within the nation will begin to heal, because they are not stirred up by those seeking to *manipulate* the masses. Under such conditions, there are no favored groups, just Americans.

And those who "allege weakness and inability" will no longer be able to count on diligent workers to pay their bills. This will result in a much-improved economic condition established, with those not truly disabled paying their own way effectively ending the economic enslavement of workers to the lazy. After much attendant conflict, which is typically associated with the masses rebelling against such masters, the *Dark Empire* will fall to the exposure of these truths, ushering in yet another *age of freedom* and enlightenment. That is the other future.

Revolution

Freedom is not won without great upheaval. This is because the ones who took it will not give it up without a fight. It is to the credit of those long ago that when the moment of decision arrived in their day they stood up to the test, securing a new *age of freedom* for many generations to come. Years later, as they one-by-one entered their beds of passing, each had the peace of knowing they had stood up to the beast of tyranny when the call came, even as fearsome as it was. And surrounded in that last moment by their loved ones, whom freedom would continue to bless, those loved ones surely reveled in their great deed.

But there is always another side to great moments, such as times when the voice of destiny calls out into a land. Those others lying in that same bed years later will contemplate the misery of not having stood up to the call in their day. And in that tender moment as their loved ones surround them, none will dare mention it.

As the *age of freedom* has passed into another *age of tyranny*, enabled by the *great dichotomy* created by the *viewing screens*, your choice is now the same. The call of destiny goes forth into the land, seeking the ears of those capable of hearing it. It is the call of the *age of freedom* that just passed, still not so far away as to return if given a way. She beckons those in whom her light was known, asking "Which of you will fight for me? Which bed will you rest in when your last moment arrives?" All face the common experience of birth and death. And when the day of the latter arrives, there ensue inevitable contemplations, a settling of accounts of one's life. You should choose to stand. And this is how.

The truths contained within this book are a cancer to the six media monoliths, and their avoidance of it will be manifest. They shall surely not promote it, nor as much as comment on it. For it undermines their carefully *created reality* of legitimacy within a "democracy." And since at its centerpiece this book promotes legislation to break their media empires apart, it is anathema to them. It is Kryptonite. Therefore,

Pass It On

Pass on this book physically and the concepts contained herein verbally to those whom might receive it, encouraging them to do the same.

And let it grow.

REFERENCES

Chapter One — "The Great Dichotomy"

1. History Places, Great Speeches Collection, Winston Churchill Speech, http://www.historyplace.com/speeches/churchill-hour.htm

Chapter Two — "In The Beginning"

1. Bradford, *Plymouth Plantation*, p 33.
2. www.History.com, "Mayflower departs England," http://www.history.com/this-day-in-history/mayflower-departs-england
3. Bradford, *Plymouth Plantation*, p 33.
4. Christopher Hilton, *Mayflower*, {Glouchestershire, England: Sutton Publishing Limited, 2005}
5. Bradford, *Plymouth Plantation*, p 95.
6. Ibid.
7. Harvey Mansfield & Delba Winthrop, Editors Introduction *Democracy in America* p xvii
8. Alexis de Tocqueville, "France in the early 19th Century" accessed 3/24/2012 http://xroads.virginia.edu/~HYPER/DETOC/democrats/ch1.html
9. Alexis de Tocqueville, *Democracy in America* p 176
10. Alexis de Tocqueville, *Democracy in America* p 177

11. Ibid.
12. Alexis de Tocqueville, *Democracy in America* p 178
13. Ibid.
14. Alexis de Tocqueville, *Democracy in America* p 282
15. Alexis de Tocqueville, *Democracy in America* p 274
16. Alexis de Tocqueville, *Democracy in America* p 275

Chapter Three — "The Foundation"

1. Kenneth Hickman, About.com Military History, "American Revolution: Battle of the Chesapeake," http://militaryhistory. about.com/od/navalbattles16001800/p/chesapeake.htm
2. www.History.com, "Battle of Yorktown," http://www.history. com/this-day-in-history/battle-of-yorktown-begins
3. Ibid.
4. Monticello.org, John Locke, http://
5. John Locke, *Two Treatises of Government*
6. The Declaration of Independence
7. John Locke, *Two Treatises of Government*
8. The Declaration of Independence
9. Ibid
10. John Locke, *Two Treatises of Government*
11. The Declaration of Independence
12. John Locke, *Two Treatises of Government*
13. Ibid
14. John Locke, Letter of Toleration
15. John Locke, *Two Treaties of Government*
16. Ibid
17. Ibid.
18. Thomas Jefferson, Letter to Roger Weighman, June 24, 1826, http://www.loc.gov/exhibits/jefferson/214.html

Chapter Four — "Age of Manipulation"

1. The Last Moments of Adolf and Eva Hitler, http:// schikelgruber.net/death.html

2. Ibid.

3. Will Stewart, *Daily Mail*, "Hitler Planned 'Big Brother' style television to broadcast Nazi propaganda," October 21, 2008, http://www.dailymail.co.uk/news/article-1079415/ Hitler-planned-Big-Brother-style-television-broadcast-Nazi-propaganda.html

4. Ibid.

5. Ibid.

6. Meredith Alexander, www.Stanford.edu, "Radio Free Europe's History of Intrigue and Information explored in Hoover Exhibit," http://news.stanford.edu/news/2001/may23/ hoover-rfe-523.html

7. Number of TV Households in America, Television History: The First 75 Years

8. www.LiveScience.com, "Could You Become a Dictator?," http://www.livescience.com/12843-dictator.html

9. Meridith Alexander, www.prisonexperiment.org, "Stanford Prison Experiment," http://www.prisonexp.org/30years.htm

10. Erin McLaughlin, www.WarBirdForum.com, "Television Coverage of the Vietnam War and the Vietnam Veteran," http://www.warbirdforum.com/media.htm

11. Zeke Turner, *The New York Observer*, "FBI Documents: Walter Cronkite Helped Organize Anti-Vietnam Protest in 69" http://www.observer.com/2010/05/fbi-documents-walter-cronkite-helped-organize-antivietnam-protest-in-69/

12. www.historycommons.org, "Context of '1969-1971: Agnew Helps Create Modern Era of Attack Politics" http://www.

historycommons.org/context.jsp?item=a6971agnewattackpoli
tics#a6971agnewattackpolitics

13. Mark Feldstein, American Journalism Review, "Watergate revisited," http://www.ajr.org/article_printable.asp?id=3735

14. Amazon.com, "Media Bias"

15. Lendol Calder, *Financing the American Dream: A Cultural History of Consumer Credit* {Princeton, NJ: Princeton University Press, 1999}pp 9

16. Ibid. pp 10

17. Ibid.

18. www.InterlectualTakeOut.org, "1952-2010 Indexed: Personal Household Debt Outstanding and Population Growth," http://www.intellectualtakeout.org/print/library/ chart-graph/1952-2010-indexed-personal-household-debt- outstanding-and-population-growth

19. Eddie M. Clarke, Timothy C. Brock, David W. Stewart, *Attention, Attitude, and Affect in Response to Advertising* {Hillsdale, NJ: Lawrence Erlbaum Associates, Inc, 1994}

20. S. Robert Lichter and Stanley Rothman, "Media and Business Elites," Media Research Center, http://archive.mrc.org/ biasbasics/biasbasics3.asp

21. Kenneth Walsh, *Feeding the Beast: The White House versus the Press* {Bloomington, IN: Xlibris Corp, 2002}

22. Media Research Center, How the Media Vote, http://archive. mrc.org/biasbasics/biasbasics2.asp

23. Samuel Lopez De Victoria, Ph.D, Psychcentral.com, "Media Manipulation of the Masses: How the Media Psychologically Manipulates," http://psychcentral.com/blog/ archives/2012/02/06/media-manipulation-of-the-masses- how-the-media-psychologically-manipulates/

24. Eddie M. Clarke, Timothy C. Brock, David W. Stewart, *Attention, Attitude, and Affect in Response to Advertising* {Hillsdale, NJ: Lawrence Erlbaum Associates, Inc, 1994}

25. Frank W. Schneider, Jamie A. Gruman, Larry M. Coutts, *Applied Social Psychology: Understanding and Addressing Social and Practical Problems* {Thousand Oaks, CA: Sage Publications, Inc, 2012} 139-148

26. Christina Bicchieri, Social Norms, "Norms and Beliefs: How Change Occurs, www.academia.edu/1596868/Norms_and_Beliefs_How_Change_Occurs

27. Frank W. Schneider, Jamie A. Gruman, Larry M. Coutts, *Applied Social Psychology: Understanding and Addressing Social and Practical Problems* {Thousand Oaks, CA: Sage Publications, Inc, 2012} 139-148

28. Christina Bicchieri, Social Norms, "Norms and Beliefs: How Change Occurs, www.academia.edu/1596868/Norms_and_Beliefs_How_Change_Occurs

29. Thomas Sowell, www.freerepublic.com, "Depending on Dependency," 9/11/12, http://www.freerepublic.com/focus/f-news/2929014/posts

30. Ibid.

31. Ibid.

32. Daniel Greenfield, Front Page Magazine, "Food Stamp Use 50% Higher Under Obama Than Under Bush," http://frontpagemag.com/2012/dgreenfield/food-stamp-use-50-higher-under-obama-than-under-bush/

33. Daniel Disalvo, National Affairs, "The Trouble with Public Sector Unions," Fall 2010, http://www.nationalaffairs.com/publications/detail/the-trouble-with-public-sector-unions

Chapter Five — "The Dark Empire"

1. James M. Wall, www.religion-online.org, "Changes in Attitude: the Lost World of the 1950s," http://www.religion-online.org/show article.asp?title=163

2. James M. Wall, www.religion-online.org, "Changes in Attitude: the Lost World of the 1950s," http://www.religion-online.org/show article.asp?title=163

3. Jennifer Buckett, "Values and morals in American society: The 1950s versus today," http://www.helium.com/knowledge/102137-values-and-morals-in-american-society-the-1950s-versus-today

4. Jonathan D. Fitzgerald, www.TheDailyBeast.com, "How TV Killed the Republican Party's Family Values," http://www.thedailybeast.com/articles/2012/11/15/how-tv-killed-the-republican-party-s-family-values.html

5. James M. Wall, www.religion-online.org, "Changes in Attitude: the Lost World of the 1950s," http://www.religion-online.org/show article.asp?title=163

6. Jennifer Buckett, "Values and morals in American society: The 1950s versus today," http://www.helium.com/knowledge/102137-values-and-morals-in-american-society-the-1950s-versus-today

7. Jonathan D. Fitzgerald, www.TheDailyBeast.com, "How TV Killed the Republican Party's Family Values," http://www.thedailybeast.com/articles/2012/11/15/how-tv-killed-the-republican-party-s-family-values.html

8. Christina Bicchieri, "Norms and Beliefs: How Change Occurs," www.academia.edu/1596868/Norms_and_Beliefs_How_Change_Occurs

9. Newton's First Law of Motion, http://www.physicsclassroom.

com/class/newtlaws/u211a.cfm

10. James M. Wall, www.religion-online.org, "Changes in Attitude: the Lost World of the 1950s," http://www.religion-online.org/show article.asp?title=163

11. Jennifer Buckett, "Values and morals in American society: The 1950s versus today," http://www.helium.com/knowledge/102137-values-and-morals-in-american-society-the-1950s-versus-today

12. Jonathan D. Fitzgerald, www.TheDailyBeast.com, "How TV Killed the Republican Party's Family Values," http://www.thedailybeast.com/articles/2012/11/15/how-tv-killed-the-republican-party-s-family-values.html

13. Eddie M. Clarke, Timothy C. Brock, David W. Stewart, *Attention, Attitude, and Affect in Response to Advertising* {Hillsdale, NJ: Lawrence Erlbaum Associates, Inc, 1994}

14. Paul Bond, *Hollywood Reporter*, TV Executives confirm Hollywood's liberal agenda," June 2, 2011, http://www.reuters.com/assets/print?aid=USTRE7517JQ20110602

15. Ibid

16. Ibid

17. Ibid

18. Ibid

19. Ibid

20. Ibid

21. Alison Motluk, *New Scientist*, "TV viewing linked to adult violence," March 28, 2002, http://www.newscientist.com/article/dn2109-tv-viewing-linked-to-adult-violence.html?full=true&print=true

22. American Academy of Child & Adolescent Psychiatry, "Children And TV Violence," March 2011, http://www.aacap.

org/cs/root/facts_for_families/children_and_tv_violence

23. Media Reform Information Center, "Number of corporations that control a majority of U.S. media," http://www.corporations.org/media/

24. Ben Shapiro, *Primetime Propaganda*, {New York, NY: HarperCollins Publishing, 2011}

25. Ibid

26. Emily Guskin and Tom Rosenstiel, The Pew Research Center's Project for Excellence in Journalism, "The State of the News Media 2012," http://stateofthemedia.org/2012/network-news-the-pace-of-change-accelerates/?src=prc-section

27. Columbia Journalism Review, http://www.cjr.org/resources/?c=ge

28. Ibid.

Chapter Six — "Ideological Cleansing"

1. Jennifer Rosenberg, History 1900s About.com, "The Nazi-Soviet Non-Aggression Pact," http://history1900s.about.com/od/worldwarii/a/nonaggression.htm

2. Ibid.

3. Ibid.

4. The United States Holocaust Memorial Museum, "The Nazi Camp System," Accessed April 29, 2012, http://www.ushmm.org/outreach/en/article.php?ModuleId=10007720

5. Gulag: Soviet Forced Labor Camps and the Struggle for Freedom, Accessed April 29, 2012, http://gulaghistory.org/nps/

6. Thomas Jefferson, Letter to Roger Weighman, June 24, 1826, http://www.loc.gov/exhibits/jefferson/214.html

7. Ben Shapiro, *Brain Washed*, {New York, NY: HarperCollins Publishing, 2004}

8. Daniel B. Klein and Charlotta Stern, "Professors and their politics: The policy views of Social scientists" 2004, http://www.criticalreview.com/2004/pdfs/klein_stern.pdf

9. Ibid

10. Ben Shapiro, *Brain Washed*, {New York, NY: HarperCollins Publishing, 2004}

11. College Confidential, "Which Colleges are the most Conservative/Liberal," http://talk.collegeconfidential.com

12. Daniel B. Klein and Charlotta Stern, "Professors and their politics: The policy views of Social scientists" 2004, http://www.criticalreview.com/2004/pdfs/klein_stern.pdf

13. Gary A. Tobin and Aryeh K. Weinberg, "A Profile of American College Faculty, Volume I: Political Beliefs & Behavior" http://www.jewishresearch.org/PDFs2/FacultySurvey_Web.pdf

14. S. Robert Lichter and Stanley Rothman, "Media and Business Elites," Media Research Center, http://archive.mrc.org/biasbasics/biasbasics3.asp

15. Kenneth Walsh, *Feeding the Beast: The White House versus the Press* {Bloomington, IN: Xlibris Corp, 2002}

16. Media Research Center, How the Media Vote, http://archive.mrc.org/biasbasics/biasbasics2.asp

17. Ibid.

18. Ibid.

19. Ibid.

20. Ibid.

21. Ibid.

22. Ibid.

23. Ibid.

24. Ibid.

25. Samuel Lopez De Victoria, Ph.D, Psychcentral.com, "Media Manipulation of the Masses: How the Media Psychologically Manipulates," http://psychcentral.com/blog/archives/2012/02/06/media-manipulation-of-the-masses-how-the-media-psychologically-manipulates/

26. Ibid.

27. Meridith Alexander, Stanford Prison Experiment: Thirty-Year Retrospective, http://www.prisonexp.org/30years.htm

28. Ibid.

29. Live Science, "Could You Become a Dictator?" http://www.LiveScience.com/12843-dictator.html

30. Ibid.

31. www.PewForum.org, Overview of Same-Sex Marriage in the United states," 12/7/12, http://www.pewforum.org/Gay-Marriage-and-Homosexuality/Overview-of-same-sex-marriage

32. Matthew J. Franck, "Supreme Court Take Notice: Two Sociologists Shift the Marriage Debate," 6/15/2012 http://www.the publicdiscourse.com/2012/06/5634

33. John Witte Jr., *The Enduring Institution: The Law of Marriage in the West* {Louisville, KY: Westminster John Knox Press, 2012}

Chapter Seven — "Divide and Conquer"

1. HistoryOfMacedonia.org, Philip of Macedon Philip II of Macedon Biography, http://www.historyofmacedonia.org/AncientMacedonia/PhilipofMacedon.html

2. Ibid.

3. Ibid.

4. Ibid.

5. Peter Roff, www.usnews.com, "Media Attacks Sarah Palin Out

of Fear She'll Become President," http://www.usnews.com/
opinion/blogs/peter-roff/2011/06/17/media-attacks-sarah-
palin-out-of-fear-shell-become-president

6. Stacy Forster, University of Wisconsin-Madison, "Study shows
    Palin treated differently by media as vice presidential candidate
    than Biden," 7/5/2012, http://www.news.wisc.edu/20852

7. Matea Gold, *Los Angeles Times*, Media on the defensive over
    Palin coverage, 9/5/2008, http://articles.latimes.com/2008/
    sep/05/nation/na-mediaattacks5

8. J. Motes, Voices, "The Sarah Palin Probe and Scandal: Media
    Bias at its Best," http://voices.yahoo.com/shared/print.
    shtml?content_type=article&content_type_id=1103063

9. Wendy Dawn, Yahoo, "CNN Shows Blatant Election Bias
    against Sarah Palin," http://voices.yahoo.com/shared/print/
    shtml?content_type=article&content_type_id=1136550

10. Douglas Mackinnon, *The New York Times*, "Media Credibility,"
    http://campaignstops.blogs.nytimes.com/2008/11/02/media-
    credibility/?page wanted=print

11. Paul Bond, *Hollywood Reporter*, "NBC News Accused
    of Editing 911 Call in Trayvon Martin Controversy,"
    3/30/2012, http://hollywoodreporter.com/news/travon-
    martin-nbc-news-editing-911-call-306359

12. Kerry Picket, *The Washington Times*, "DOJ on New Black
    Panther Party Zimmerman bounty-No Comment," http://
    www.washingtontimes.com/blog/watercooler/2012/mar/30/
    doj-new-black-panther-party-zimmerman-bounty-no-co/

13. Cathy Grossman & Richard Wolf, *USA Today*, "Bishops,
    Obama in church-state faceoff over birth control,
    2/12/2012, http://www.usatoday.com/news/washington/
    story/2012-02-12/obama-bishops-contraceptives/53065070/1

14. Jeffrey Jones, Gallup Organization, "Gender Gap in 2012 Vote Is Largest in Gallup's History," http://www.gallup.com/poll/158588/gender-gap-2012-vote-largest-gallup-history.aspx

15. Tom Cohen, www.CNN.com, "Obama administration to stop deporting some young illegal immigrants," 6/16/2012, http://www.cnn.com/2012/06/15/politics/immigration/index.html

16. Phillip Elliott & Dennis Junius, *Huffington Post*, "Obama Gay Marriage Announcement Does Little To Shift Views: AP Poll, 6/22/2012, http://www.huffingtonpost.com/2012/06/22/obama-gay-marriage-poll_n_1618180.html

17. Reid Epstein, *Politico*, "Obama Touts student loan bill," 7/7/2012 http://www.politico.com/news/stories/0712/78193.html

18. David Barstow, *The New York Times*, "Tea Party Lights Fuse for Rebellion on Right," http://www.nytimes.com/2010/02/16/us/politics/16teaparty.html?pagewanted=all

19. Dylan Byers, www.politico.com, "ABC News apologizes for incorrect report." 7/20/2012 http://www.politico.com/blogs/media/2012/07/abc-news-tea-party-connection-incorrect-129588.html

20. Los Angeles CBS Local, "MTV Star Claims Alleged Aurora Theater Shooter Called Him Prior To Massacre, http://losangeles.cbslocal.com/2012/08/01/mtv-star-claims-alleged-aurora-theater-shooter-called-him-prior-to-massacre/

21. Ibid.

22. Ibid.

23. Edith Honan, *Chicago Tribune*, "Occupy movement's May Day turnout seen as test for its future," http://articles.chicagotribune.com/2012-05-01/news/sns-rt-us-usa-occupy-

may1bre84001e-20120430_1_protesters-plan-security-precautions-labor

24. Mary Kate Cary, www.usnews.com, "What's Hidden in Obama's Julia Campaign," http://www.usnews.com/opinion/blogs/mary-kate-cary/2012/05/04/whats-hidden-in-obamas-julia-campaign

25. Historic Words, "John Adams-Our Constitution Was Made Only For A Moral And Religious People," http://historicwords.com/american-history/john-adams-our-constitution-was-made-only-for-a-moral-and-religious-people/

26. Ibid.

27. Benjamin Rush, *Thoughts Upon The Mode Of Education Proper In A Republic*, Philadelphia, 1786

28. L. Gordon Tait, *The Piety of John Witherspoon: Pew, Pulpit, and Public Forum*, Westminster John Knox Press, 2001, pp 160

29. David Brooks, *The New York Times*, "If It Feels Right..." September 12, 2011, accessed June 2012, http://www.nytimes.com/2011/09/13/opinion/it-it-feels-right.html?pagewanted=print

30. Ibid

31. *The New York Times*, "The Moral Values of America's Youth," September 15, 2011, accessed June 2012, http://www.nytimes.com/2011/09/16/opinion/the-moral-values-of-americas-youth.html

32. Jon Ward & Joshua Hersh, Democrats' Efforts To Reinsert 'God' And 'Jerusalem' in Platform Met With Loud Opposition," 9/7/2012, http://www.huffingtonpost.com/2012/09/05/dnc-god-jerusalem-platform_n_1859200.html

MANIPULATING MAN

Chapter Eight — "The Rise of the Drones"

1. "Radio Listeners in Panic, Taking War Drama as Fact," *The New York Times*, 31 October 1938, p. 1, 4.
2. Ibid
3. Roger Manville, Heinrich Fraenkel, *Heinrich Himmler: The SS, Gestapo, His Life and Career*, Skyhorse Publishing Inc., 2007 Google Print, p.76
4. Ibid
5. Hugo Dixon, Reuters, "Cyprus deposit grab sets bad precedent," 3/17/2013, http://blogs.reuters.com/hugo-dixon/2013/03/17/cyrpus-deposit-grab-sets-bad-precedent/
6. *The Washington Times*, "Editorial: From Arab Spring to Islamist Winter," 10-25-11, http://www.washingtontimes.com/news/2011/oct/25/from-arab-spring-to-islamist-winter/print/
7. Mary Kate Cary, www.USNews.com, "What's Hidden in Obama's 'Julia' Campaign," http://www.usnews.com/opinion/blogs/mary-kate-cary/2012/05/04/whats-hidden-in-obama
8. Rebecca Williams, www.Criminology.fsu.edu, "Philip Zimbardo: A psychologist's experiment with deviance," Summer 1998, http://www.criminology.fsu.edu/crimtheory/zimbardo.htm
9. Ibid.
10. Ibid.
11. Ibid.

Chapter Nine — "Witches and Rogues"

1. Discovery Education, "Salem Witch Trials," http://school.discoveryeducation.com/schooladventures/salemwitchtrials/people/proctor.html

2. Ibid

3. Radiostratosphere.com, "RADIO IN THE 1930s," http://www.radiostratosphere.com/zsite/behind-the-dial/radio-in-1930.html

4. Gary He, *The New York Times*, "Rush Limbaugh," 3/5/2012, http://topics.nytimes.com/top/reference/timestopics/people/l/rush_limbaugh/index.html

5. Matthew Smith, Yahoo! Voices, "Left Wing Attack on Rush Limbaugh's Free Speech," http://voices.yahoo.com/shared/print.shtml?content_type=article&content_type_id=9408758

6. Ibid.

7. Peter B. Collins, Truthout, An Insider's View of the Progressive Talk Radio Devolution, 2/10/13, http://truth-out.org/opinion/item/14355-an-insiders-view-of-the-progressive-talk-radio-devolution

8. Columbia Journalism Review, http://www.cjr.org/resources/?c=ge

9. Dylan Matthews, *The Washington Post*, "The Sequester: Absolutely everything you could possibly need to know, in one FAQ, 2/20/2013, http://www.washingtonpost.com/blogs/wonkblog/wp/2013/02/20/the-sequester- Absolutely-everything-you-could-possibly-need-to-know-in-one-FAQ

10. David Jackson, *USA Today*, "Obama Blames Rebublicans for sequester," http://www.usatoday.com/story/news/politics/2013/03/02/obama-republicans-sequester-cathy-rodgers/1958019/

11. Mark Felsenthal, Reuters, "Journalist Woodward tangles with White House over spending cuts," 2/28/2013, http://www.reuters.com/article/2013/02/28/us-usa-fiscal-woodward-idUSBRE91R0T020130228

12. Ibid.

13. John Nolte, Breitbart, How Woodward's Truths and Sullivan's Smears Expose Our Corrupt Media," 3/12/2013, http://www.breitbart.com/Big-Journalism/2013/03/13/Woodward-Sullivan-Media

14. Mark Felsenthal, Reuters, "Journalist Woodward tangles with White House over spending cuts," 2/28/2013, http://www.reuters.com/article/2013/02/28/us-usa-fiscal-woodward-idUSBRE91R0T020130228

15. Ibid.

16. Tanner Colby, www.Slate.com, "Regrettable," 3/12/2013, http://www.slate.com/articles/arts/culturebox/2013/03/bob_woodward_and_gene_sperling_what_woodward_s_john_belushi_book_can_tell.html

17. Alex Pareene, www.Salon.com, "Bob Woodward demands law-ignoring, mind-controlling presidential leadership," http://www.salon.com/2013/02/27/bob_woodward_demands_law_ignoring_mind_controlling_presidential_leadership/

18. Dan Gainor, www.foxnews.com, "Liberal Media attacks as Woodward 'threat' seen as political threat to Obama," http://www.foxnews.com/opinion/2013/03/01/left-attacks-as-woodward-threat-seen-as-political-threat-to-obama/

19. Ibid.

20. Matthew Hindman & Kenneth Cukier, *The New York Times*, "More News, Less Diversity," 6/2/03, www.nytimes.com/2003/06/02/opinion/more-news-less-diversity.html?pagewanted=print&src=pm

21. Kenny Olmstead, Jane Sasseen, Amy Mitchell & Tom Rosenstiel, The Pew Research Center's Project for Excellence in

Journalism, "Digital: News Gains audience but Loses Ground in Chase for Revenue,"

22. Ibid.

23. Julie Moos, Poynter., "The Top 5 news sites in the United States are…" www.poynter.org/latest-news/mediawire/128994/the-top-5-news-sites-in-the-united-states-are/

24. Ibid.

25. John Hawkins, RightWingNews.com, "The 50 Most Popular Conservative Websites," http://www.rightwingnews.com/uncategorized/the-50-most-popular-conservative-websites/

26. Terry Frieden, CNN, "Holder does not rule out drone strike scenario in U.S.," http://www.cnn.com/2013/03/05/politics/obama-drones-cia

27. Mark Judge, Real Clear Politics, "Our Nixonian Press," 2/23/13, http://www.realclearbooks.com/articles/2013/02/23/our_nixonian_press_44.html

28. Ibid.

29. Ibid.

30. Ibid.

31. Ibid.

32. Ibid.

33. Rep. Lamar Smith, The Daily Caller, "The Media's President," http://dailycaller.com/2010/09/04/the-medias-president/?

34. Ibid.

35. Dan Gainor, www.Foxnews.com, "ABC, NBC and CBS ignore union thugs' attack on Fox News contributor," 12/12/12, http://www.foxnews.com/opinion/2012/12/12/abc-nbc-and-cbs-ignore-union-thugs-attack-on-fox-news-contributor/

36. Patrick Howley, TheDailyCaller.com, "CNN journalist criticizes liberal media bias in Jana Winter case," http://dailycaller.com/2013/04/08/cnn-journalist-criticizes-liberal-media-bias-in-jana-winter-case/

37. www.WashingtonTimes.com, "Are Liberal media attacking conservatives?" 06/26/2011 http://communities.washingtontimes.com/neighborhood/porter-politics/2011/jun/26/are-liberal-media-attacking-conservatives/

38. Kristen Powers, www.FoxNews.com, "Obama vs. Fox News—behind the White House strategy to delegitimize a news organization," 01/29/2013 http://www.foxnews.com/opinion/2013/01/29/obama-vs-fox-news-behind-white-house-strategy-to-delegitimize-news-organization/

39. Ibid.

40. Ibid.

41. Ibid.

42. Ibid.

43. Emily Guskin and Tom Rosenstiel, stateofthe media.org, "State of the Media 2012—Network: By the Numbers," http://stateofthemedia.org/2012/network-news-the-pace-of-change-accelerates/network-by-the-numbers/

44. Uri Friedman, www.theatlanticwire.com, "Why Cable News is Shedding Viewers," http://www.theatlanticwire.com/business/2011/03/why-cable-news-shedding-viewers/35820/

45. Peter Roff, www.usnews.com, "Media Attacks Sarah Palin Out of Fear She'll Become President," http://www.usnews.com/opinion/blogs/peter-roff/2011/06/17/media-attacks-sarah-palin-out-of-fear-shell-become-president

46. Stacy Forster, University of Wisconsin-Madison, "Study shows Palin treated differently by media as vice presidential candidate

than Biden," 7/5/2012, http://www.news.wisc.edu/20852

47. Matea Gold, *The Los Angeles Times*, Media on the defensive over Palin coverage, 9/5/2008, http://articles.latimes. com/2008/sep/05/nation/na-mediaattacks5

48. J. Motes, Voices, "The Sarah Palin Probe and Scandal: Media Bias at its Best," http://voices.yahoo.com/shared/print. shtml?content_type=article&content_type_id=1103063

49. Wendy Dawn, Yahoo, "CNN Shows Blatant Election Bias against Sarah Palin," http://voices.yahoo.com/shared/print/ shtml?content_type=article&content_type_id=1136550

50. Eric Owens, Daily Caller, "Florida Atlantic issues new groveling aology over Jesus-stomping," http://dailycaller. com/2013/03/27/florida-atlantic-issues-new-groveling-apology-over-jesus-stomping-video/

51. Beth Kassab, www.OrlandoSentinel.com, "Point missed on Jesus-stomping lesson at FAU," http://articles.orlandosentinel. com/2013-03-27/features/os-beth-kassab-jesus-stomping-lesson-20130327_1_jesus-students-focal-point

52. Ed Morrissey, www.HotAir.com, "Scott to FAU: Explain this Jesus-stomping indicent to me, please," http://hotair. com/archives/2013/03/27/scott-to-fau-explain-this-jesus-stomping-incident-to-me-please/

53. Matthew Smith, Yahoo! Voices, "Left Wing Attack on Rush Limbaugh's Free Speech," http://voices.yahoo.com/shared/ print.shtml?content_type=article&content_type_id=9408758

54. "The Obama File," http://the obamafile/_associates/ obamaassociates.htm

55. *Free Republic*, "Obama's Questional Associates," 7-20-2008 http://www.freerepublic.com/focus/bloggers/2048657/ posts

56. Matthew Smith, Yahoo! Voices, "Left Wing Attack on Rush Limbaugh's Free Speech," http://voices.yahoo.com/shared/print.shtml?content_type=article&content_type_id=9408758

57. Joe Newby, Examiner.com, "MSNBC caught editing clip from rally to attack Mitt Romney," 9/28/2012, http://www.examiner.com/article/msnbc-caught-using-edited-clip-from-rally-to-attack-mitt-romney

58. Ibid

59. Bryan Preston, PJMedia.com, "MSNBC Caught Doctoring Video to Attack Romney," 9/28/2012, http://pjmedia.com/tatler/2012/09/28/msnbc-caught-doctoring-video-to-attack-romney/

60. John Hayward, *Free Republic*, "Death Threats leveled against Rush Limbaugh," 3-8-12, http://freerepublic.com/focus/f-news/2856272/posts

Chapter Ten — "Tyranny!"

61. Pamela Kline, www.revolutionary-war.new, "The Olive Branch Petition," http://www.revolutionary-war.new/olive-branch-petition.html

62. History.com, "King George refuses Olive Branch Petition," http://www.history.com/this-day-in-history/king-george-refuses-olive-branch-petition

63. Shmoop.com, Politics in The American Revolution, "The French, the Indians, and the Americans," http://www.shmoop.com/american-revolution/politics.html

64. John Locke, *Two Treatises on Government*

65. Shmoop.com, "Politics in The American Revolution," http://www.shmoop.com/anerican-revolution/politics.html

66. Chuck Braman, "The Political Philosophy of John Locke

and Its Influence on the Founding Fathers and the Political Documents They Created," http://www.chuckbraman.com/writing/writingfilesphilosophy/locke.htm

67. John Locke, *Two Treatises on Government*
68. The United States Constitution
69. Ibid
70. Thomas Jefferson, www.famguardian.org, Letter to William Green Munford," http://www.famguardian.org/subjects/Politics/Thomas Jefferson/jeff1600.htm
71. Encyclopedia Britannica Profiles, Thomas Jefferson, http://www.britannica.com/presidents/article-9116908
72. Alexis de Tocqueville, *Democracy in America*
73. Thomas Jefferson, Letter to Roger Weightman, 6-24-1826, http://www.loc.gov/gov/exhibits/jefferson/214.html
74. Thomas Paine, *Common Sense*, http://www.fordham.edu/halsall/mod/Paine-common.asp
75. John Locke, *Two Treaties on Government*
76. Ibid
77. Ibid
78. Ibid
79. Ibid
80. Ibid.
81. Ibid.
82. Ibid.
83. Ibid.

Chapter Eleven — *"Achilles"*

84. James Hunter, Achilles, Encyclopedia Mythica, http://www.pantheon.org/articles/a/achilles.html
85. Ibid.

86. Ibid.

87. Ibid.

88. Laura Fitzpatrick, Stockholm Syndrome, Time, 8/31/2009, http://www.time.com/time/magazine/article/0,9171,1920301,00.html

89. Lymari Morales, U.S. Distrust in Media Hits New High, Gallup, http://www.gallup.com/poll/157589/distrust-media-hits-new-high.aspx?

90. Ben Shapiro, *Primetime Propaganda*, {New York, NY: HarperCollins Publishing, 2011}

91. Encyclopedia Britannica Profiles, Thomas Jefferson, http://www.britannica.com/presidents/article-9116908

92. Thomas Paine, *Common Sense*, http://www.fordham.edu/halsall/mod/Paine-common.asp

93. Ibid.

94. Alexis de Tocqueville, *Democracy in America*

95. Ibid.

96. Thomas Jefferson, Letter to Roger Weighman, June 24, 1826, http://www.loc.gov/exhibits/jefferson/214.html

www.ingramcontent.com/pod-product-compliance
Lightning Source LLC
LaVergne TN
LVHW051508080426
835509LV00017B/1984